Civil War Soldiers

IN THE HEART OF CLARK CO., WISCONSIN

Presented by the Clark Co., WI History Buffs

© 2009
ISBN-13 978-0-9840764-0-6
ISBN-10 0-9840764-0-9

http://wvls.lib.wi.us/ClarkCounty/
Visit us for additional information about our veterans and local history.

In Memory of Greenwood, Wisconsin's
CIVIL WAR SOLDIERS

John A. Eaton Post #213, Grand Army of the Republic 30 May 1907

From left, top row: William Oelig, Paschel Wallis, William Harrison Mead, John Scovel, John Foust, John McCarty and Tom Vine.
Lower row: John Booth, Jess Crane, Paul Rossman, Charles Richelieu and Charles Cummings.

Check our web site for updated and additional information.

http://wvls.lib.wi.us/ClarkCounty/

PREFACE

The Clark County History Buffs first organized in July of 2001 with a small but faithful group of volunteers dedicated to preserving the history of Clark County, WI, on the World Wide Web. For lack of funding, a brick and mortar county-wide history center has never been established. Our group has attempted to fill this void with a pioneer effort to provide a digital library collection which is open twenty-four hours a day, 365 days a year. Today we have over a hundred members and an extensive database used by researchers all over the world.

This book was compiled from the website materials which are now available to anyone with a computer and a love for history. It is dedicated to the memory of the Civil War Soldiers who are buried in the Greenwood, WI City Cemetery and to those who once resided in and around Greenwood, WI, including the townships of Beaver, Eaton, Warner and Weston. We have no way of knowing how many of these veterans belonged to the formal organization known as the Grand Army of the Republic which is often referred to as the G.A.R. Therefore, we have included as many as possible under the assumption that many did belong, if only for a short time, to the John A. Eaton post #213. Obviously we may have included veterans who were not affiliated with the Greenwood organization, but all did reside in one of the four townships which are clustered together in the heart of Clark County, WI.

Those who have donated funding, thoughts and ideas, photographs, family records, endless hours of transcribing, proof-reading, artwork, restoring old photos, researching and time to contact families and visit their homes are too numerous to mention. Without them, this book would never have come to be. We thank them all for their unbelievable dedication to the completion of this project. Special acknowledgements go to Al Wessel for his outstanding documentation, to Paul Forster for researching and purchasing military documents, to Dolores Kenyon for proof-reading, to Lani Bartelt, Deb Sanger, Crystal Wendt, Ken Wood and Marla Zwakman for their dedication to accurate research, to Sharon Short and Marsha Hosfeld for their help with writing, editing and compiling, to Chuck Debevec for his mapmaking skills and proof-reading and to Dick Adler for organizing the funding and promotion of this project. The profits from this book will be used by the Greenwood American Legion to replace the time worn and missing markers in the Greenwood City Cemetery for the veteran soldiers who are in need of them.

It would be out of place to insinuate that our soldiers did better than any others, but it is fair to say they did their full duty, used their best skills and sometimes gave their lives on the battlefield or lived with physical injuries throughout the remainder of their days. It is our hope that the following pages will give you a new appreciation of the price they paid to preserve the union of the United States and to demolish the outrageous practice of slavery.

Obviously, it was impossible to include everything we uncovered concerning these veterans; therefore we invite you to visit our WI Valley Library System website if you would like to know more or if you have additional information to share.

Webmasters, Janet & Stan Schwarze
http://wvls.lib.wi.us/ClarkCounty/

TABLE OF CONTENTS

Abbreviations

Art'y=artillery, b.=birth, dates following proper names with no designation can be assumed to be birth dates, btry.=battery (artillery), BN=Battalion, ca=circa or approximately, Capt.=Captain, Co.=County, Co.=Company, Cpl= Corporal, d.=death/died, G.A.R.=Grand Army of the Republic, H. A.=Heavy Artillery, Inf.=Infantry, I.O.O.F.=International Organization of Odd Fellows, L.A.=Light Artillery, Lt = Lieutenant, m.=married, M.E.=Methodist Episcopal, M.O.= Mustered Out, Maj.=Major, O.G.= Officer of the Guard, Q.M.= Quartermaster, Reg.= Regiment, Sgt. = Sergeant, Twp.=Township, sometimes used following a place name instead of the original "Town of " which always preceded the identities: "Town of Eaton" vs. Eaton Twp., U.S.=United States, U.S.N.=United States Navy, Vet = Veteran, VGR=Veteran Grave Registration, yrs.=years

⚑ **Indicates the soldier is buried in the Greenwood, WI City Cemetery.**

☆ **Indicates the soldier belonged to the Grand Army of the Republic (G.A.R.)**

A Name in bold within a biography indicates that person is also featured in this book.

*VGR: L. A. Allen of Neillsville oversaw the veteran's graves registration work for the county and followed up the work even after the government called off the project before its completion. The Clark Co. Register of Deeds holds his work. Veterans buried in the county before 1938 were recorded. An example form is included in the first biography.

Brief History of the Grand Army of the Republic

☆
IOWA
OHIO
MAINE
VERMONT
NEWYORK
INDIANA
KENTUCKY
CONNECTICUT
NEBRASKA
RHODE ISLAND
PENNSYLVANIA
CALIFORNIA
NEW HAMPSHIRE
WISCONSIN
MINNESOTA
MASSACHUSETTS

The Union Pyramid, 1863 (published in the Northern States)

The "G.A.R." was forged 6 Apr 1866 by Benjamin. F. Stephenson in Decatur, IL, from the lasting friendships which had grown between the soldiers, sailors, and marines honorably discharged from their service in preserving the *United* States of America. At peak membership in 1890, the organization numbered 409,489 veterans who served between 12 Apr 1861, and 9 Apr 1865. These enduring souls founded soldiers' homes and were active in relief work and pension legislation. To honor those who had not lived to return to civilian life, they encouraged the establishment of national military cemeteries and the marking of graves. The May 30th celebration of Memorial Day began in 1868 with the issuing of a General Order by their Commander-in-Chief, John A. Logan. The Women's Relief Corps developed as an auxiliary to the G.A.R. Five members were elected President (Grant, Hayes, Garfield, Harrison and McKinley) and, for a time, it was impossible to be nominated on the Republican ticket without the G.A.R. voting block's endorsement. The final Encampment of the Grand Army of the Republic was held in Indianapolis, IN during 1949 and its last member, Albert Woolson, died in 1956 at the age of 106.

History of the John A. Eaton G.A.R., Post #213
Established in Greenwood, WI, 20 Oct 1885; disbanded 1919

John A. Eaton, named for his paternal grandfather, was born 11 Mar 1848, the son of Ebenezer and Hannah (Cross) Eaton of Newbury, Merrimac Co, NH. His siblings were: Phineas (1836); Albert S. & Alfred S. (13 Aug 1841-twins); Jesse Wilbur F. (8 Apr 1843); Edwin A. (16 Apr 1846 m. Margaret, a sister of **John A. McCarty**); and Phineas A. Eaton (3 Nov 1856). John enlisted in the NH Union army as a private on 9 Aug 1862. He was promoted to Full 1st Sgt. He re-enlisted with Co. H, 10th NH Inf. 4 Sep 1862, and was quickly promoted to Full 2nd Lt., 9 Jun 1863. On 1 Jan 1864, he was promoted to Full 1st Lt. That spring he died from the wounds he suffered at the battle for Cold Harbor, 27 May 1864.

The Battle of Cold Harbor and the Death of John A. Eaton

Before the Civil War, shelter (harbor) for weary travelers was provided at Burnett's Cold Harbor Tavern which stood on a crossroads in the heart of rural Virginia, about 2 mi. E of Gaines' Mill and 10 mi. S of Richmond, the confederacy capital. Far removed from anything resembling a port for ship docking, *Cold Harbor* became the point where streams of soldiers from the North intersected with the military flow from the South. In 1862, these armies assaulted one another until the fields were soaked with blood at the "First Battle of Cold Harbor." Two years later, Lt. Gen. Ulysses S. Grant's Army prepared to battle Gen. Robert E. Lee's forces in the "Second Battle of Cold Harbor."

←While digging their preparatory trenches, the soldiers were disturbed to uncover the skeletal remains from the first conflict. Locals have claimed the ghostly battles are still raging and can be heard most mornings about 1 a.m. The smell of gunpowder still lingers in the air and the fields are thought to be haunted by a little girl who fell from the window of the grave keeper's house. Her ghost is said to have been heard both laughing and crying while wandering the lonely cemetery at Mechanicsville-Cold Harbor.

John A. Eaton was mortally wounded before the crossing of the Pamunkey River during the onset of this second slaughter, but his brother, **Alfred S. Eaton**, continued to fight on with their New Hampshire Regiment. A head-on attack 3 Jun 1864 against a narrow section of the line cost the Union Army 7,000 casualties in half an hour. Although Grant's troops suffered these unprecedented losses, he himself never visited Richmond. In his memoirs he wrote, "I have always regretted that the last assault at Cold Harbor was ever made. I might say the same thing of the assault of the 22nd of May, 1863, at Vicksburg. At Cold Harbor no advantage whatever was gained to compensate for the heavy loss we sustained."

The **John A. Eaton Post ledger** has many missing pages but does contain the minutes of most monthly meetings spanning 11 Mar 1905 through 13 Jan 1917 in a standard format: *"Post opened in due form with Commander (name) in the chair. Minutes of last meeting read and approved as read. Q.M. report: cash on hand (amount). No further business coming before the Post it was closed in due form. Signed (name) Adjutant"* Election of officers was held in December with the formal installation ceremony taking place the following January.

13 Jan 1917 Officers

Paul **Rossman**, age 73, d. 1918
Charles **Cummings**, age 75, d. 1926
William **Oelig**, age 76, d. Nov 1917
John **Blecha**, age 77, d. 1926
William **Dutcher**, age 80, d. 1926
Jessie **Crane**, age 90, d. 1922
John **Hoffman**, age 72, d. 1923
Paschel **Wallis**, age 76, d. 1922
John **Booth**, age 77, d. Jan 1919
Frank **Able**, age 71, d. 1922
Fred **Buker**, age 76, d. 1924
Carl **Richelieu**, age 78, d. Nov 1917

Interesting notations: 13 April 1907 **"Jack Stevens** and **John Booth** appointed on committee for refreshments for the Old Boys on Decoration Day."** 27 Feb 1909 "The following Comrades signed for the Lincoln Centennial Medal" [list of 17 names]. 2 Nov 1912 "Some of the Confederate money was given to all Comrades present."

During the early years this was followed by a "bountiful" supper prepared by some of the wives of the members who then joined them in a celebration meal. There were eleven officers elected on a yearly basis: Post Commander, Senior Vice-commander, Junior Vice-commander, Adjutant, Surgeon, Chaplain, Q.M., Officer of the Day, Officer of the Guard, Sergeant Major, Q.M. Sergeant plus a Trustee who was appointed for 3 years. In 1913 "In-site Sentinel" and "Out-site Sentinel", and in 1915 "Patriotic Instructor" were added as officer positions. **R. S. Hummel** was Post Commander in Mar 1905. He resigned the following month and transferred his membership to the Neillsville Post. Thereafter, **Paul Rossman** was Post Commander, except for a few months in 1908 when he "went west". Other officer from 1905-1917 were: **Tom R. Vine, William Dutcher, John Booth, Jesse C. Crane, T. L. Pratt, Carl Richelieu, John Foust, John Sanford, John Blecha, John A. Scovel, Charles Henry Cummings, William Oelig, Paschel Wallis, John Tatro,**

Zephaniah Silvers, Christian Wollenberg, Frank Abel, Fred Buker, Sr., **John H. Hoffman, Abram H. Shoemaker. John McCarty** was a "Trustee". Other member names found in the ledger were: **Joe Gibson, Jack L. Stevens, and Henry Decker.** When a member died the Post Charter was draped for 30 days, presumably in a black cloth or sash.

The **G.A.R.** in Greenwood, Eaton Twp., Clark Co., WI was named for **John A. Eaton**, the brother of Alfred Surraneous Eaton who was among the founding members when it was established in 1885. A. S. Eaton became one of Wisconsin's best-known Civil War veterans. "Maj. Eaton" was a former State Commander of the G.A.R. and active in Masonic circles as well. The earliest history of Post 213 has been obscured by time and little documentation exists concerning it. We do know its monthly meetings were announced in the local paper, The Greenwood Gleaner, in a column called "Secret Societies." The July 2, 1903 notice to the left tells us the group met on a bi-monthly basis at 2 o'clock on the second and fourth Saturday afternoon of each month. At this time, Paul Rossman served as the Post Commander and John W. Daugherty was the Adjutant.

Looking Back at a Traditional Celebration

1908 Memorial Day Parade, Greenwood, WI

"Decoration Day was always looked forward to with a program in the hall. The G.A.R., the band and the schoolchildren always marched to the cemetery where the children decorated the graves of the soldiers. At first the programs were held in the Begley Opera House and "Uncle George" Andrews always made the speech. Those of later days are held in the Opera House. The old soldiers of the Civil War marched in the procession year after year until only one was left. When he became too old to carry the flag, John Arends, a veteran of the Spanish-American war, carried it for him. The G.A.R. once held a reunion at the school grounds lasting 3 days. The soldiers ate and slept in tents, made speeches, sang war songs, and told of their experiences. Some well known members of the G.A.R. were: Alfred S. **Eaton**, George **Meek**, Francis **M. Carter**, Rudolph S. **Hummel**, Ebulius G. **Hartson**, Lary **Drinkwine**, Charles H. **Cummings**, Jesse C. **Crane**, Frank **Abel**, Thomas **R. Vine**, Carl **Richelieu**, Henry **Decker**, William **Oelig**, Joseph **Gibson**, Chris **Wollenberg**, Moses **Babb**, John **Sanford**, August **Nagel**, Hiram **W. Varney**, John **A. McCarty**, Caleb W. **Chandler**, Joseph **Palmer**, Fred G. **Sheldon**, Paul **Rossman**, Paschel **Wallis,** and John **Booth**. There are no Civil war veterans left in this community but the only Spanish-American veteran and the young soldiers of the World's War now march in the procession on Decoration Day, the school children and the band still take part--old band members usually returning for the occasion. Last year, for the first time, the high school band took part and last Decoration Day a reunion for old band members and old settlers was held on Mrs. Burch's lawn. It was well attended and much enjoyed by all present." *Greenwood, Hub of Clark Co.,, Wis."*

Brief History of the American Civil War

The Civil War took more American lives than any war in history. When 11 states defied government authority 20 Dec 1860 by withdrawing from the 34 state union, a Confederate capital was established in Richmond, VA—within shooting distance of Washington, D.C. where Lincoln was inaugurated 4 Mar 1861. The first shots of the 4 year war were fired in Charleston, SC. It ended when Gen. Robert E. Lee surrendered his ragged, exhausted army to a hard driving, cigar-chewing Gen. U. S. Grant at the Appomattox, VA, Court House, 9 Apr 1865. Approximately 700,000 Americans had died and the Southern way of life, dependent upon slave labor, was destroyed. The question of whether a state could secede from the union was answered. The war introduced us to land-mines, breech-loading and repeating rifles, telescopic sights, railroad artillery, photographed battle accounts and press correspondents, balloon observation, organized medical and nursing corps, hospital ships, the U.S. Secret Service, the income tax, withholding tax, tobacco taxes, The Medal of Honor, the bugle call "Taps", the first African-American Army officer (Major M. R. Delany), the gray-uniformed Southern soldier dubbed *Johnny Reb* (Rebel) and the blue-uniformed *Billy Yank* (Yankee), and the first assassinated American President, Abraham Lincoln.

Wisconsin raised 91,200 soldiers divided into regiments of about 780 each, organized into 10 Companies—53 Infantry units (4 composed of Germans), 4 cavalry, a company of Berdan's sharpshooters, 13 light artillery batteries and 1 heavy artillery unit. The distinguished **Iron Brigade**—the 2nd, 6th, 7th Wis., 19th Ind. and the 24th Mich.—wore Hardee hats and long frock coats. During their baptismal battle on a hillside at Brawner's Farm the brigade lost more than 900 of its 2,100 men. Previous to this engagement, only the 2nd Wis. had seen combat. During the cornfield battle of Antietam the Black Hat unit proudly led the way. The 6th Wis. was under the direction of Major Dawes who told how they were "loading and firing with demoniacal fury… shouting and laughing hysterically." That one battle led to deaths of more than 8,000 Americans. In McPherson's Wood during the Battle of Gettysburg, when the fearsome I Corps was spotted by the confederates, a shout went up, "There are those damned black-hatted fellows again!" During the blood bath the Union army captured the Confederate's Gen. Archer. Shortly after the next sunrise Major Gen. Doubleday greeted him, "Good morning, Archer." Prisoner Archer replied, "Well, I am *not* glad to see you—by a damned sight." At the battle of McPherson's Ridge the 1,829 man Iron Brigade suffered 1,153 casualties before falling back to Seminary Ridge. A Confederate officer later heard the howling of wounded and said, "I approached some with the purpose of calming them if possible. I found them foaming at the mouth as if mad." Shortly afterward the Confederates attacked again and a Union cannoneer described the scene, "men reeling and falling; splinters flying from wheels and axles where bullets hit; in rear, horses tearing and plunging, mad with wounds or terror; smoke, dust, splinters, blood, wreck and carnage indescribable." Unable to sustain anymore, the Iron Brigade broke and fled.

Co. "C", 2nd WI Infantry Volunteers wearing their Hardee hats
Capt. Geo. W. Gibson-Lt. Wm. Booth-Lt. J. A. Kellogg, standing in order to the far left.

Some Clark County soldiers who fought with these regiments were: Allen N. Jeremiah, Romeo Bostwick (Cav), John Davis (Cav), William **Dutcher**, John Ferrell, R. Hoel (Cav), Frank Jarvis, Enoch Johnson (Cav), M. Kapka (Bat.), Loran Murray Johnson, Gabriel Adolphus Lupient, William Henry **Marden**, W. Mathison, George Maynard, Truman McIntyre (Cav), Gorman Muller, George I. Oatman, John Ferell, August Pierrelle (Cav), M. M. Post (Cav), A. Preston (Cav), George Robinson (Cav) and Herman Sweager (Cav), all from the **2nd Wis.** Those from the **6th Wis.** were: Charles Burnett, A. B. Day, Fredrick Gambort (Bat), James Garnet (Cav), C. Healy (Cav), Charles Harding (Cav), Charles Huesler, Joseph Alonzo Janes, James Joseph, Hiram Kayhart, Richard Lester, Calvin Mills, James C. Moody, William Palmer, Martin Schultz, Guilford Smith, Sylvester Elmer Perry **Sweet**, James Tilden and Steven D. Tuttle. Our soldiers from the **7th Wis.** were: Stillman H. **Benjamin**, Alexander Cross, George Follet, Milo Hanks, A. McHugh, Benson **Peck**, Hiram W. Soper and Mathias N. Wells (Bat). Those from the **24th Mich.** were: W. H. Daily, Peter F. **Lantz** and Andrew N. Virch.

Wisconsin's first regiments were outfitted in impressive gray uniforms, but the Federal Gov. ordered they be replaced with the regular army blue. Critical eyebrows were raised when the state had to pay a second time for "sleazy" replacements. The first 10 companies of 3 month volunteers gathered at Camp Scott near Milwaukee. Later recruits were sent to Camps Barstow, Bragg, Douglas, Hamilton, Harvey, Holton, Salomon, Threadway, Utley and Washburn, but most companies were sent to the State Agricultural Society fairgrounds near Madison to be housed in the stables, cowsheds and tents. Many new recruits fell ill after sleeping on flea ridden straw pallets and eating spoiled beef. This place was later named "Camp Randall." The first 1,260 Confederate prisoners captured on Island #10 in the Mississippi River were held there from April-June 1861. After a month, 94 of them had died of disease and uncared for wounds. While guarding that camp, the 19th Wis. plundered many supplies intended for prisoners. Even after adequate bedding was sent, 200 or more ill prisoners languished on the bare floor of the "hospital" — the former "Floral Hall" of the fairgrounds had become a bed of hell.

As early as mid-1861, a fur trader offered up 500 Chippewa braves and another white man offered 200 Menominee braves as recruits but Lincoln declined. The Indians as a whole were excluded from Civil War service until 1864 when 279 braves from Wisconsin's Menominee, Oneida and Stockbridge reservations were accepted as Union soldiers. Nine Wisconsin Regiments accompanied Grant on his bloody Wilderness campaign in northern VA. When the survivors of the Army of the Potomac arrived below Richmond July 30, 1864, a tremendous mine was set to break the Confederate lines outside of Petersburg. Charging ahead was Co. K of the 37th Wis., consisting mostly of Menominee Indians and Co. F of the 29th Wis. US Colored troops. These newly recruited Indians and Negroes went into the heavily mined crater, only to be trapped. That day 85 of those soldiers died. Of the 250 men in the Company, only 95 answered roll call that evening and 57 laid dead or dying.

In 1863, except for those it discharged as unfit for further service, the army ceased to allow the sick and wounded a furlough, instead keeping them in military hospitals, some as far south as New Orleans. In October 1863 through the efforts of Mrs. Harvey and a petition signed by 8,000 Wisconsinites, those needing medical attention were allowed to go to a hospital in their home state. Throughout the war, soldiers who were discharged for disabilities made their way homeward. Thousands of soldiers, sick, disabled, or destitute, were compelled to beg for food, lodging and transportation home. Milwaukee and Madison were designated as the places where troops received their final payment and discharge. Most of these men were encamped near Washington and transferred to Louisville, KY, before being shipped northward, many in boxcars or on flatcars. *Adapted from "The History of WI" by Richard N. Current Volume II, The Civil War Era, 1848-1873*

How Soldiers Were Drafted

In 1860, 750,000 people were living in WI. Draftees and volunteers combined, it sent 92,000 to southern battlefields out of 240,170 who were of an eligible age. All males from 18 to 45 years were liable. The call for the first draft was received by Gov. Salomon Aug. 5, 1862. A draft drawing took place at the courthouse in Milwaukee Nov. 19. The 9 wards of the city were subject to a draft of 10,888. Twenty-four cigar boxes sat in a double row on a large table in the court house with each town or ward in the county allotted 2 apiece. One contained the names of all subject to draft in the district and the other the names of those exempt. The contents were poured into a larger box and the names were drawn from it by a small blind-folded boy who couldn't read or write. The day of the drawing the court house was surrounded by an armed guard and only the officials were admitted inside. The anxious wives, mothers or sweethearts of those subject to the draft and those liable themselves waited in the square. As a district was completed the names of those chosen for duty were announced to the throng outside. A total of 4,537 names were drawn. Of these 988 were discharged, 19 deserted, 1,662 failed to report and only 1,739 were mustered in. So many volunteered to fill old regiments that only 1 new regiment was filled by the draft. This was the 34th WI and after lying in camp here until 31 Jan 1863, it was ordered to Columbus, KY, on fatigue duty. When it returned to Milwaukee it had lost 20 by death, 283 had deserted, 186 were discharged and 472 were mustered out. The 2nd draft took place in Milwaukee, Nov 1863. It called for 3 of every 10 eligible recruits. This accounted for all males from 20 to 45 years of age, divided into 2 groups. The males from 20 to 35 years of age and all unmarried men over 35 years of age and under 45 years comprised the 1st group. The married men from 35 to 45 years of age were in the 2nd group. The draft was to be made from the first classification and the second class was exempt. The draftee could escape service by paying $300. Another draft came in July 1864. This time there was no escape by the payment of commutation fee. Every man drawn had either to serve himself or hire a substitute and many of the eligible draftees desperately searched for a "sub." The office of the examining physicians was crowded to capacity day and night. The History of Milwaukee says: "Never before had the city shown such a display of disease. It seemed the entire military population was undergoing a diagnosis. One half seemed suddenly stricken and the other half disclosed chronic ailments heretofore suffered in silence. A maimed hand or foot became a great boon, and hernia, sufficient to obtain exemption, was deemed a blessing. Happy was he who lacked a toe or wore a truss." Cowards who failed to report, packed trunks and left for Canada and parts unknown, only to return after the war to enjoy the fruits of peace and prosperity with their cash still in hand. A brisk and profitable business was done by substitute brokers. Those who hired a substitute were fortunate. As always, it was the poor man that suffered. Lacking the money to hire someone else, he had to wait around until taken. Quotations on the "sub" market began at $100 per year of service required and subsequently went as high as $800. In later drafts nearly everyone of military age served because substitutes became impossible to find. *Adapted from the Milwaukee Evening WI, 9 Jun 1917.*

Civil War Military Record of Clark Co., WI

There were about 120 families living within its borders when Clark Co., WI responded to President Lincoln's call for volunteers to aid in suppressing the rebellion of the Southern States. With a total population of some 800 people, it furnished about 30 men to the 14th Wis. Vol. Infantry. Their recruits were all enrolled for 3 years with Co. I. An able lawyer and good soldier, Capt. Calvin R. Johnson of Black River Falls, initially served as their commander. Less than 30 days after leaving the state in early March 1862, the 14th Wis. suffered bloodshed during the battle of Shiloh. In all it lost 100 soldiers who were killed, hospitalized or captured. Gottlieb Schlinsog from the town of Grant was mortally wounded and Charles G. Bacon (1842) later died from his injuries. Charles was a son of Orson Bacon, a pioneer settler of Pine Valley. The G.A.R. Post at Neillsville was named in his honor. Eight months later the regiment lost another 95 men at the battle of Corinth. The 14th Wis. was with Grant at Vicksburg in 1863. During a charge before that city in May they sustained the loss of 107 men. On the surrender of Vicksburg the regiment was given the post of honor and led the advance of the troops on their entry into the surrendered city. They went on the Red River expedition and part of regiment was with Gen. Sherman in his Atlanta campaign.

Early in 1865 they were sent to New Orleans, and shortly afterward fought at Spanish Fort until its surrender, and were in various skirmishes along the coast of the Gulf of Mexico. They were not mustered out until 9 Oct 1865, about 6 mos. after Lee's surrender to Grant at the Appomattox Court House. In his memoirs Gen. Sherman noted that Wisconsin kept her regiments filled, whereas other states tended to meet their quotas by adding new regiments. He estimated one Wisconsin regiment equaled a brigade (a 3 to 4 fold strength).

Shiloh Meeting House

The following members of Company I, 14th Wis. Inf., resided in Clark Co., WI, at the time of their enlistment: Gustave R. Ayers, *Charles Bacon, Charles F. Bone, Chauncey Blakeslee, Wilson S. Covill, Hy G. Chamberlain, Benjamin Darling, Charles W. Foote, James W. Ferguson, Benjamin Folsom, Alexander Green, Edward Houghton, Joseph Ives, John F. King, George R. King, *Louis Lynch, Edward H. Markey, Andrew J. Manley, William Neverman, *John O'Neill, Nelson Osgood, *Henry Ross, Robert F. Sturdevant, John R. Sturdevant, *Washington Short, Gottlieb Schlinsog, Cyrus O. Sturgeon, **Thomas Vine**, Ferdinand C. Wage and *Thomas Whitmore.

*Denotes the Clark Co., WI, members of Co. I, who were killed, died of wounds, or lost their lives by disease in the South in the line of duty.

Louis Lynch of Neillsville was one of James and Margaret (Kirkland) Lynch's 11 children. **John O'Neill** was a son of James O'Neill, the founder of Neillsville. **Washington Short** who married Lydia Green was the father of 3 small children. **Henry Ross** was the brother of Robert Ross, a lumberman from Ross' Eddy. Young Gottlieb **Schlinsog** (1846 ca.) was a son of Carl and Anna (Neltner) Schlinsog of Grant Twp. In **1909** there were only 10 veterans from Co. I, 14th Wis. still living: Wilson S. **Covill** was in the hotel business at Olympia, WA [sheriff of Clark Co., 1869 - 1870 and married Isabella S. O'Neill, oldest daughter of James O'Neill and first white child born in the county]; James **Ferguson** who had a hardware business at Wenatchee, WA; George R. **King**, a son of George W. King of Humbird; Thomas R. **Vine** of Warner [moved to Idaho in 1910, buried there]; Joseph **Ives** was living at the Soldiers' Home near Portland, OR; Edward **Houghton** of Tacoma, WA [lived at Houghtonburg, WI, before the war and was elected Clark Co. treasurer in 1860]; John "Rufe" **Sturdevant** of Neillsville [Served as D. A., Judge, and Court Commissioner for the Circuit Court of Clark Co., WI]; Robert S. **Sturdevant** of Olympia, WA [served as Register of Deeds and D. A. for Clark Co. and held the offices of State's Attorney and District Judge in WA]. The Sturdevant brothers were sons of James W. Sturdevant, a founding father of Neillsville, WI.

"Oct. 9, 1866, the Clark Co. veterans held their first reunion at the Hubbard House in Neillsville, it being the first anniversary of their muster-out. W. T. **Hutchinson** spoke and war stories were shared along with a supper, music and dancing. After 2 or 3 similar annual reunions, the guest list was broadened to include all of the area's veterans, irrespective of what company or regiment they had served. At another reunion a cannon the 14th Wis. had captured at the battle of Shiloh was borrowed from Madison and a sham battle was fought a 1/4 mile southeast from the Neillsville high school. Louis **Sontag** and James **Delane** were in charge of the piece when carelessness caused a premature discharge and Delane lost one of his arms. Some of the affairs where quite elaborate. Maj. George W. **Hubbel**, Capt. George **Austin** and Capt. Tom **La Flesh** would mount their prancing steeds to ride at the head of the parading military company. This along with speeches by the old soldiers generally made such a celebration a red-letter day for the community.

The Sick, Dying and Wounded

Near every major battlefield both sides picked out a "Dying Tree." The mortally wounded spent the last moments of their lives in the shade of those trees surrounded by the agony of other dying soldiers and within earshot of the horrifying warfare. All Civil War Medics were designated *Surgeons*, regardless of their experience with a scalpel. They did the best they could in impossible situations but their ghastly record of success underscored the vastness of their task. More soldiers died of illness than from enemy fire.

Yellow fever is transmitted by mosquitoes, but the physicians of the Civil War days attributed it to other causes. One Confederate doctor actually shipped clothing worn by victims of it to the

17

northern cities in an effort to spread the disease to the union towns. Even Lincoln was slotted to receive "infected" shirts in hopes he'd be taken by the fever. As many soldiers were claimed by dysentery as were killed by bullets. Plagues of measles are known to have postponed battles. Field hospital surgeons commonly amputated limbs without sanitation. Heaps of arms and legs were a common site at the field hospitals. The chilling, repetitive sound of the bone saws and the groans of the injured were all too familiar to the ambulance corps. Opium was occasionally used as a painkiller and many wounded soldiers became addicted to it. Because supplies were always low, many unfortunate boys received nothing whatsoever to dull the pain before the removal of a limb. If the ill and injured survived the field hospitals they were taken to general hospitals like Charles G. Bacon of Neillsville who went to Jefferson Barracks where he died. Gangrene and a wide range of infections threatened wounded who were hanging by a thin thread of life. Sometimes after their battle for life was lost their mutilated bodies were shipped back to their grieving families. But, as the National Cemeteries records indicate, most were buried near were they died.

1863 Letter to Home

John Henry Welsh was born 12 Jun 1843, the son of Uri and Rhoda Kilbourn Welsh in Steuben Co, NY. In 1846 the family moved to Shabbona Grove, De Kalb Co, IL, where his mother died. His father moved Henry and his little brother back to Wisconsin to be near relatives. A year later Uri also died and his parents took the two little boys, Henry, five and Albert, three. Henry lived with them in Iron Ridge, WI, until he was seventeen. On April 15th, following the attack on Ft. Sumter, President Lincoln called for a volunteer army of 75,000 men for three months' service. A week later young Henry was sworn in as a private in the 1st Wis. Volunteers' Army. After his discharge in August he reenlisted, this time for three years service in Co I, 29th Wis. Inf. Army pay was $13.00 a month, and like most of the boys, Henry sent an allotment home. In a few months time he was promoted to sergeant. On June 26, 1863, Sgt. Welsh was wounded at Vicksburg by a mini-ball, and spent the next six weeks in Geosha Hospital at Memphis, TN. After a short furlough at home, he was back in action... In war and in peace, this gallant gentleman served his country until his death on February 24, 1918. *Compiled by Mildred Mack Sterr, Contributed by Sherrin Mack*

(The following John Henry Welsh's letter is to his grandmother, not his mother)

Dear Mother   Helena, Ark March the 13th, 1863

As I had time I thought I would write you o few lines to let you know that I am well, and hope that these few lines will find you the same. I have received my boots all right. The right one is plenty large enough, but the left one is pretty small but I think it will be all right after I have worn it a few times. The boys are all well that come from the Ridge that are here, but Sam Torbert and Ed Cole are both dead. I tell you it is hard; there has three died that inlisted at the Ridge. We have lost nine out of our company and they all had the mesles but one. Thare haint but one had the mesles that got over them and that was Orin Chet. His mother told him to drink cold water if he got them and he done so and got well. But the rest drank warm tea and such stuff and caught cold and died; but he would not drink enything warm altho the doctor said he should. But he would not and so you see he got well. I tell you if a man gets sick here and has to go to a hospital he never comes out alive ..- or ten changes to one he doesnt. But if he will take care of himself and doctor on roots and bark and such stuff, he will get well in a few days. He wants to keep himself clean and exercise himself in pitching quoits or playing ball. I tell you that just as soon as a man dont fell very well he will go in his tent and lay thare from morning till night; that haint what he wants to do. What he wants to do--he wants to stir around and exercise himself a little every day. And some bring on sickness by eating too much and then lye down and not ster. I tell you that is the cause of a good meny men dying. But lust as long as I can ster, I will If I dont feel able to walk, I will get a horse and ride. I have a chance to be as sick as eny of them. Thare was a week that I felt pretty bad, but I went on fatigue and picket and then we went down to the Yazoo Pass. We had to march six miles. I might have had a horse to ride, but I would not. The next day I went and helped kill a beef. The next day after I felt all right again, when. if I had given up I might have been a pretty sick fellow by now. I will not take the doctors medisin. I believe it does a man more hurt than good. I am getting fat and George Sifts is as fat as Ernest Whelock used to be; I will bet he wighs over two hundred pounds. Nute Allen is getting fat. Some men will get fat while others grow poor. Some men the climate agrees with better than others; It agrees with me first rate I tell you.

There was a man read in a Memphis paper to day that the 29th was ordered to Utah. How true it is I don't know, but it is reported as a fact; they say that the Mormans are raising and that we will have to go and put them down. I hope it is so, but I cant hardly believe it yet. Dave Laup wanted me to write to you and ask if you could spar Albert to go and do his choars untill it was warm weather enough for the cattle to pick their own livin. If Frank wants to hire out, let him go thare; Dave said he would pay him what was right; he cant get eny one to do his choars. I tell you it is too bad here he is down here and cant get home to do them himself and cant get eny one to do them for him. If one of them will go I will risk bet that he will pay them what he said he would. Albert Visgar is well but Charley - I don't know eny thing about him only he's at Vicksburg, or thare about a diging land some whare and he is well. Dave Gripes is pretty sick; he is from Watertown. Ari knows him. He was taken just the same as Charley McDupper was. Leon Crandal is well.

Now I want you to answer this as quick as you get it. I hove gat my picture taken and you will find it in this letter. Look at it and see if it looks enything like I used to and see if it looks like a soldier. I cant think of eny more to write. You must write and tell me if either of the boyes will go to Daves or not. How much do you think that picture cost? Well, I will tell you--it cost one dollar--a pretty good price I tell you! You must get it put in a case if you want one for I could not send it in a case. You will have to excuse the poor writing and bad spelling--no more at preasant.

Yours truly,, Henry Welsh

Please write soon. Give my Love to all inquiring Friends, H W

Civil War Veterans Residing in Clark Co., WI in 1885

SOURCE: **CENSUS REPORT - 1885** - WI ENUMERATION of SOLDIERS and SAILORS of the LATE WAR Residing in **Clark** County, **WI**, June 20, 1885. This census, like many of the old census records, was very difficult to read because of the faded ink and fancy penmanship. The phonetic spelling of many surnames caused transcribers to take their best guess. Every attempt was made to ensure that all Clark Co Civil War Veterans were included in the following list according to where their mail was received. Underlined entries = buried in Greenwood Cemetery.

Present day **TOWN OF BEAVER** est. 1870
TERRO Post Office

HUTCHINS, W. W. *Pvt., Co. G, 39th WI* **ROMAINE**, EDWARD W. *Pvt., Co. C, 14th WI* **SMITH**, GUILFORD *Sgt., Co. E, 6th WI*

Present day **TOWN OF COLBY** est. 1873
COLBY Post Office

BARTELL, W. H. *Pvt., Co. B, 11th WI* **BECHERER**, A. *Pvt., US Vessel* **BRYANT**, J. H. *Pvt., Co. C, 16th VT* **BULLOCK**, D. S. *Sgt., Co. B, 1st WI Cav.* **COLLINS**, AMBROSE *Drum Major Co. A, 48th WI* **COLLINS**, W. W. *Pvt., Co. G, 32nd WI* **DAILEY**, J. W. *Pvt., Co. A, 21st WI* **EDER**, GEO. *Pvt., Co. A, 1st Art. WI* **FAILEY**, GEO. F. *1st Sgt., Co. K, 3rd WI* **FANCHER**, CHAS. *Pvt., Co. B, 11th NY* **GRAMBORT**, FRED *Pvt., 2nd Btry. 1st Art. WI* **GRAY**, ALBERT *Pvt., Co. I, 1st WI* **HABERSETZER**, LEONARD *Pvt., Co. I, 14th WI* **JARVIS**, FRANK *Pvt., Co. B, 2nd WI Cav.* **MARSH**, EDWIN *Pvt., Co. F, 86th NY* **McCARTHY**, PAT *Pvt., Co. D, 27th WI* **McCARTHY**, WM. *Cpl., Co. G, 14th MI* **PRESTON**, A. J. *Pvt., Co. E, 2nd WI* **SIEBER**, JACOB *Pvt., Co. H, 3rd WI* **SIEGRIST**, H. *Musician Co. G, 14th WI* **STEINEBACH**, PETER *Pvt., Co. A, 4th US Cav.* **TAYLOR**, C. R. *Pvt., Co. C, 1st WI Cav.* **WELSCH**, H. *Pvt., Co., M, 26th WI* **WILMS**, B. A. *Pvt., Co. G, 21st WI*

Present day **TOWN OF EATON** est. 1869
GREENWOOD Post Office

ABEL, FRANK *Pvt., Co. F, 48th WI* **AUSTIN**, W. G. *Pvt., Co. C, 19th WI* **BABB**, MOSES *Pvt., Co. D, 20th WI* **BLECHA**, JOHN *Pvt., Co. I, 34th WI* **BUKER**, FRED *Cpl., Co. C, 27th WI* **CHANDLER**, C. W. *Pvt., Co. G, 5th WI* **COATS**, F. M. *Pvt., Co. D, 11th WI* **CRANE**, JESSE *Pvt., Co. B, 179th PN* **CUMMINGS**, CHAS. *Pvt., Co. C, 30th WI* **DARLING**, M. *Pvt., Co. C, 1st WI* **DECKER**, HENRY *Pvt., Co. C. 23rd, WI* **DRINKWINE**, LARY *Pvt., Co. B, 8th WI* **EATON**, A. S. *Pvt., Co. H, 10th NH* **FIELDS**, ALFRED *Pvt., Co. A, 33rd, WI* **HOGUE**, C. P. *Pvt., Co. H, 10th WI* **HUMMEL**, R. S. *Pvt., Co. Co,. G, 10th WI* **HUBBELL**, GEO. W. *Pvt., Co. C, 179th PN* **McCALVY**, ROBERT *Pvt., Co. G, 14th WI* **MARKHAM**, CURTIS *Pvt., Co. A, 35th IN* **NEWTON**, C. W. *Pvt., Co. G, 1st WI* **NICHOL**, ROBERT *Pvt., Co. D, 33rd WI* **OELIG**, WM *Pvt., Co. G, 14th WI* **RICHLIEU**, CARL *(WI unit unknown)* **ROSSMAN**, PAUL *Pvt., Co. A, 9th WI* **RUFINOT**, LOUIS *Pvt., Co. K, 4th WI Cav.* **RUFINOT**, *FRANK Pvt., Co. ?, 49th WI* **SANFORD**, JOHN *Pvt., Co. I, 76th PN* **SMITH**, GEO. W. *Pvt., Co. K, 4th WI* **STEEL** THOS. *Cpl., Co. C, 4th WI* **THOMAS**, H. J. *seaman, "Dictator" U.S. Navy* **VINE**, THOS. *Pvt., Co. I, 14th WI* **WOLLENBURG**, *CHRIS Pvt., Co. L, 5th U.S. Art.*

Present Day **TOWN OF FREMONT** est. 1874
SNOW Post Office

CLARK, ALBERT *Pvt., Co. O, 32nd WI* **DOW**, WENTWORTH *Pvt., Co. E, 16th WI* **EASTMAN**, CHARLES F. *Pvt., Co. H, 12th NH* **FIKE**, IRA *Pvt., Co. C, 94th NY*, **HEATH**, MARTIN *Pvt. Co. A, 106th NY* **HOVER**, ALLEN *Pvt., Co. M, 3rd PE Bat.* **OATMAN**, GEO. I. *Pvt., Co. E, 2nd WI* **PHILIPPE**, JASON *Pvt., Co. E, 16th WI* **SNOW**, HARVEY *Pvt., Co. B, 13th MI* **SWEET**, RALPH *Pvt., Co. H, 18th WI* **TERRELL**, JOHN *Pvt., Co. E, 2nd, 16th WI* **WEBSTER**, E. A. *Drummer, Co. K, 13th MI*

Present day **TOWN OF GRANT** est. 1868
MAPLE WORKS Post Office

CANFIELD, JOHN *Pvt., Co. B, 12th NY H Art.* **CHASE**, HORACE S. *Pvt., Co. A, 1st WI Cav.* **CONRAD**, SIGMOND *Pvt., Co. F, 52nd NY* **DAVIS**, T. W. *Pvt., Co. B, 16th NY* **GERZMAHL**, WM. *Pvt., Co. G, 34th WI* **HAGOR**, EMIL B. *(Confederate) Co. F, 1st LA* **HARDING**, WM. *Pvt., Co. L, 1st WI H. Art.* **LEONARD**, HENRY L. *Pvt., Co. F, 12th WI* **LOHMAN**, JOSEPH *Pvt., Co. D, 49th WI* **MARSH**, NELSON *Pvt., Co. C, 3rd, WI* **MOH**, CHRISTIAN *Pvt., Co. A, 1st WI* **OBER**, H. H. *Pvt., Co. A, 92nd NY* **OSGOOD**, L. B. *Pvt., Co. H, 16th NY* **PIERRELLE**, AUGUST *Pvt., Co. D, 2nd WI Cav.* **STEINFELDT**, JOHN *Pvt., Co. B, 27th WI* **SUTHERLAND**, JOSEPH *Pvt., Co. I, 13th NY Cav.* **SWEAGER**, HERMAN *Pvt., Co. A, 2nd WI Cav.* **TARBOX**, CHAUNCEY D. *Pvt., Co. D, 4th WI* **TOWNS**, HENRY H. *Pvt., Co. F, 94th NY, Sgt., Co. F, 84th NY* **WILLIAMS**, ELY *Pvt., Co. A, 53rd WI* **WILLIAMS**, JOHN *1st Sgt., 25th IL*

PLEASANT RIDGE Post Office

BRAATZ, RICHARD *Pvt., 2nd WI Bat.* **BROOKS**, GEO. *Pvt., Co. I, 3rd WI* **HUESLER**, CHAS. *Pvt., Co. F, 6th WI* **KUECHENMEISTER**, CHAS *Pvt., Co. A, 45th WI* **SLOCOMB**, CHAS *Pvt., Co. A, 18th WI* **WEST**, GEO. *Pvt., Co. H, 3rd WI* **WILDING**, GEO. Jr. *Pvt., Co. I, 1st WI Cav.*

Present day **TOWN OF HIXON** est. 1880
WITHEE Post Office

GILBO, JOHN *Pvt., Co. F, 3rd NY* **GILBO**, JOSEPH *Pvt., Co. G, 1st MI* **KRAMER**, JOHN *Pvt., Co. B, 38th WI* **MEEK**, THOS. *Pvt., Co. H, 48th WI* **MILLER**, JOHN W. *Seaman "Constellation"* **MOODY**, JAMES C. *Sgt., & Brevet Capt., Co. I, 6th WI* **NEVEL**, JAS. *Pvt., Co. K, 1st NM* **OLESON**, MICHAEL *Pvt., Co. A, 3rd WI*

Present Day **TOWN OF HOARD** est. 1873
CURTISS Post Office

BRISBOIS, GABRIEL *Pvt., Co. C, 1st U.S. Cav.* **DARROW**, H. A. *Pvt., Co. G, 6th OH Cav.* **HICKCOCK**, GEO. C. *Pvt., Co. C, 5th NY Cav.* **LARSON**, LOUIS *Able Seaman U.S.S. Junietta* **LUPIENT**, GABRIEL ADOLPHUS *Pvt., Co. G, 2nd WI* **MULLER**, GORMAN *Pvt., Co. A, 2nd WI* **MUNSON**, J. C. *Sgt., Co. D, 15th WI* **VIRCH**, A. N. *Pvt., Co. E, 24th MI* **YOUNGER**, ANDREW *Pvt., Co. L, 3rd WI Cav.*

Present Day **TOWN OF LEVIS** est. 1856
DAY Post Office

BABCOCK, D. G. *Pvt., Co. K, 38th WI* **CROCKETT**, BENJAMIN *Pvt., Co. L, 16th ME*

Present Day **TOWN OF LONGWOOD** est. 1895
LONGWOOD Post Office

DAVIS, BENJAMIN *Pvt., Co. ? 18th WI* **DOTY**, FRANCIS M. *Pvt., Co. C, 19th MI* **GIBSON**, JOSEPH *Pvt., Co. G, 12th WI* **LANTZ**, PETER F. *Pvt., Co. D, 24th MI* **McCARTY**, JOHN *Pvt., Co. C, 49th WI* **MAYNARD**, GEO. Pvt. *Co. A, 2nd WI* **MEAD**, WM. *Pvt., Co. A, 3rd WI* **MORRIS**, DANIEL *Pvt., Co. F, 44th WI* **REDWINE**, JAMES *Pvt., Co. H, 86th IN* **SHELDON**, FREDERICK J. *Sgt., Co. B, 2nd MI*

Present Day **TOWN OF LOYAL** est. 1865
LOYAL Post Office

ALLEN, DANIEL *2nd Sgt., Co. K, 1st WI* **ALLEN**, I. N. *Pvt., Co. I, 29th WI* **ARMS**, JAS. *Pvt., Co. D, 153 NY* **ARMS**, JOSEPH *Pvt., Co. E, 3rd, WI* **BAKER**, J. *Pvt., Co. C, 37th WI* **BART**, JAS. *2nd Sgt., Co. E, 21st WI* **BORDEN**, EBENEZER *Pvt., Co I, 3rd WI* **BRASIER**, J. F. *Pvt., Co. I, 16th WI* **CANNON**, HORACE *Pvt., Co. I, 14th WI* **CATLIN**, AARON, *Pvt., 10th WI Bat.* **CHESTERMAN**, J. W. *2nd Lieut., Co. A, 6th MI H. Art.* **CHURCHILL**, OLIVER *Pvt., Co. H, 92nd IL* **DRAPER**, H. *Pvt., Co. B, 166th OH* **DUTCHER**, WM. *Pvt., Co. K, 2nd WI* **HILTON**, Wm. H. *Pvt., Co. A, 16th U.S.*, **HODGE**, WM. *Pvt., Co. D, 44th WI* **HUNTER**, ISAAC A. *Pvt., Co. G, 48th WI* **KINNE**, D.J. *Pvt., Co., K, 5th MN* **LEATHERDALE**, L. *Pvt., Co. A, 11th IL* **LEROY**, L. *1st Sgt., 1st NY Sharp Shooter* **LUM**, JAMES K. *Pvt., Co. H, 11th WI* **LYON**, J. W. *Pvt., Co. A, 31st WI* **LYON**, JOHN *Pvt., Co. I, 29th WI* **MERRILL**, CHAS. *Pvt., Co. I, 29th WI* **MILES**, W.T. *Pvt., Co. B, 22nd WI* **MOLIGAN**, OLIVER *Pvt., Co. G, 5th WI* **NICHOLS** CHAS. *Pvt., Co. H, 31st WI* **NAGEL**, AUGUST *Pvt., Co. G, 34th WI* **OLESON**, ALEX *Pvt., Co. G, 5th WI* **PHILPOTT**, TOM *Hospital Steward, Co. A, 29th WI* **PRIOR**, ALBERT K. *Pvt., Co. C, 50th WI* **RICE**, E. *1st Cpl., Co. K, 75th IL* **ROGERS**, DAVID R. *Pvt., Co. H, 14th WI* **ROSSMAN**, FRED *Pvt., Co. D, 9th WI* **SALISBURY**, JOHN *Pvt., Co. A, 151st IN* **SHAVER**, JAS. *Pvt., Co. H, (reg.? WI)* **SHAVER**, NORM *Pvt., Co. F, 37th WI* **SMITH**, C. A. *1st Sgt., Co. E, 8th WI* **SMITH**, VOLNEY *Pvt., Co. B, 16th WI* **STEVENS**, S. S. *Pvt., Co. I, 27th WI* **VAN CAMP**, E. G. *Pvt., Co. F, 43rd WI* **WELSH**, ALBERT *2nd Cpl., Co. B, 52 WI Cav.*

Present day **TOWN OF LYNN** est. 1862
LYNN Post Office

GEARY, JOHN *Pvt., Co. D, 18th WI* **HOOVER**, JOHN *Pvt., Co. C, 25th NY Cav.* **JOHNSON**, VALENTINE *Pvt., Co. E, 11th PN* **LEY**, JOHN *Pvt., Co. H, 21st WI* **MOULDENHAUR**, MIKE *Pvt., Co. A, 26th WI* **WELCH**, STEPHEN *Pvt., Co. F, 12th WI*

Present day **TOWN OF MAYVILLE** est. 1889
ABBOTSFORD Post Office

JACOBSON, JULIUS *Pvt., Co. C, 28th WI*

DORCHESTER Post Office

BARTON, JOHN *Pvt., Co. A, 19th U.S.* **BLAISDELL**, A. M. *Pvt., Co. F, 92nd NY* **CENTER**, DAVID *Pvt., Co. G, 153rd NY* **COLLIER**, H. J. *Pvt., Co. E, 5th WI* **CUMMINGS**, JOHN *Pvt., Co. D, 107th NY* **HANKS**, MILO *Pvt., Co. A, 7th WI* **HOMSTED**, AUGUST *Paymaster, Steward U.S.S. Gennessee* **HUGABOOM**, HOSIA *Pvt., Co. E, 16th WI* **KRAKENBERGER**, JOHN *Pvt. Co. C, 27th WI* **KUCKERBOCKER**, WALTER *Pvt., Co. E, 21st MI* **LANSWORTH**, J. J. *Sgt., Co. C, 15th WI* **LUCIA**, THOS. *Pvt. Co. K, 20th WI* **MATHISON**, W. *Pvt., Co. G, 2nd WI* **OBERBILLIG**, MATHIAS *Cpl., Co. H, 24th WI* **OLDER**, H.M. *Lieut., Co. A, 15th IL* **PLUNKETT**, J. A. *Pvt., Co. G, 37th WI* **SCHOOLCRAFT**, MILES *Pvt., Co. K, 32nd WI* **STEPHENS**, S. T. *Pvt., Co. H, 32nd WI* **TOURTELLOTTE**, A. J. *Pvt., Co. I, 3rd WI Cav* **TUTTLE**, S. D. *Sgt., Co. E, 6th WI* **WAGNER**, JOHN *Pvt., Co. E, 9th U.S.* **WINCHELL**, ALBERT *Cpl., 8th WI Bat.*

Present day **TOWN OF MENTOR** est. 1866
HUMBIRD Post Office

BANKER, HENRY *Pvt., Co. E, 12th WI* **BENNETT**, J. C. *Pvt., Co. D, 1st WI Bat.* **BUTTERFIELD**, JOHN *Pvt., Co. B, 11th NY* **CAMPBELL**, WM. *Pvt., Co. I, 45th IL* **CARMAN**, ELI *Pvt. Co. A, 14th OH* **COMSTOCK**, CHARLES *Pvt., Co. A, 18th WI* **COMSTOCK**, W. M. *Pvt., Co. F, 1st U.S. Eng.* **DELAPP**, EPHRAIM *Pvt., Co. B, 107th NY* **DOUGLAS**, CHAS. *Pvt., Co. F, 1st WI H. Art.* **EDWARDS**, C. C. *1st Sgt., Co. F, 106th NY* **FRADENBURG**, GEO. S. *Pvt., Co. C, 75th IL* **GLEASON**, G. W. *Pvt., Co. K, 60th NY* **HARTMAN**, WM. *Pvt., Co. B, 16th WI* **HICKMAN**, HENRY *Pvt., Co. K, 11th MN* **HOUGHTON**, E. P. *Cpl. Co. I, 14th WI* **KING**, GEO. R. *Pvt., Co. I, 14th WI* **McCLAFLIN**, ELISHA *Pvt., Co. M, 4th WI Cav.* **McFARLAND**, M. H. *Pvt., Co. M, 5th OH. V.C.* **NETTLETON**, CYRUS *Pvt., Co. I, 14th WI* **PAGE**, J. *Pvt., Co. E, 1st ME H. Art.* **PETERSON**, ANDREW *Pvt., Co. B, 102nd IL* **PHALEN**, E. K. *Pvt., Co. F, 48th WI* **PURNELL**, JOHN *Pvt., Co. H, 48th WI* **SMITH**, A. L. *Pvt., Co. H, 1st MN H. Art.* **STANLEY**, ADDISON *Cpl., Co. D, 109th NY* **STANLEY**, ANSON *Pvt., Co. C, 5th NY* **STILES**, C. W. *Pvt., Co. A, 50th NY* **STILES**, HORACE *Pvt., Co. G, 36th PE* **WEBSTER**, B. *Drummer, Co. I, 31st WI* **WOODWARD**, M. F. *Pvt., Co. A, 161st NY*

AUGUSTA (Eau Claire Co.) Post Office

REDFIELD, WARREN A. *Pvt., Co. L, 1st WI Heavy Art*

FAIRCHILD (Eau Claire Co.) Post Office

BOWMAN, JOSEPH *Pvt., Co. K, 14th WI* **QUICK**, J. R. *Pvt., Co. H, 37th WI* **SHANKS**, THOS. *Pvt., Co. L, 1st WI Heavy Art*

Present day **TOWN OF PINE VALLEY** est. 1853
NEILLSVILLE Post Office

ADKINS, WM. *Pvt., Co. F, 35th WI* **ALDRICH**, WM. *Pvt., Co. F, 4th WI Bat.; Co. F, 6th U.S. Cav.* **ALLEN**, C. N. *Pvt., Co. H, 16th NY* **AUSTIN**, G. A. *1st Lieut., Co. A, 15th IL* **AUSTIN**, VOLNEY *Pvt., Co. I, 3rd NY* **BALLOW**, ALVA *Pvt., Co. C, 10th WI* **BARNES**, J. V. *Pvt., Co. I, 20th WI* **BEARDSLEY**, GEORGE L. *Pvt., Co. I, 4th WI* **BLANCHARD**, FREEMAN S. *Pvt., Co. F, 11th NH* **BROTHERS**, J. D. *Pvt., Co. I, 42nd WI* **BROWN**, E. B. *Pvt., Co. E, 20th MI* **BROWN**, JACOB *Pvt., Co. I, 50th WI* **BULLARD**, A. J. *Pvt., Co. D, 12th WI* **BULLARD**, GEORGE *Pvt. Co. I, 27th WI* **BURNETT**, CHAS. *Pvt., Co. G, 30th WI Co. I, 27th WI* **BURNS**, JAS. *Pvt., Co. L, 1st IL* **BUTTERFIELD**, Jos. *Pvt., Co. A, 1st U.S. Eng* **CALL**, IRA E. *Pvt., Co. F, 13th NY Cav.* **CAMPBELL**, WM. B. *Pvt., Co. H, 38th WI* **CARNEY**, BARNEY *Pvt., Co. C, 19th U.S.* **CARR**, I. T. *Pvt., Co. G, 42nd WI* **CHAMBERLAIN**, H. G. *Pvt., Co. I, 14th WI* CHRISTMAS, JOHN H. *Cpl., Co. G, 12th MI* **COOK**, JOHN *Pvt., Co. B, 44th WI* **COOK**, M. M. *Pvt., Co. E, 29th OH* **CORZETT**, J. S. *Pvt. Co. B, 46th WI* **COVILL**, W. S. *Pvt., Co. I, 14th WI* **CROSS**, ALEXANDER *Pvt., Co. A, 7th WI* **DAVIS**, ABNER *Pvt., Co. G, 22nd WI* **DAVIS**, SOLON *Pvt., Co. D, 12th WI* **DAY**, A. B. *Cpl., Co. G, 6th WI* **DAY**, JEDIDAH *Pvt., Co. C, 7th CA* **DELANE**, JAMES *Pvt., 1st WI Bat.* **DELANE**, PETER *Pvt., Co. I, 24th MA* **DICKINSON**, DECATUR *Pvt., Co. I, 45th WI* **DIXON**, SAMUEL *Pvt., Co. C, 57th IN* **DOUSE**, WM. *Pvt., Co. A, 18th WI* **DRAKE**, FRED *Pvt., Co. D, 96th NY* **ENHELDER**, J. K. *Pvt., Co. G, 10th WI* **FARGO**, CHAS. B. *Pvt., Co. P, 1st WI Cav.* **FERGUSON**, JAMES *Pvt., Co. I, 14th WI* **FENELSON**, GEORGE *Pvt., Co. A, 14th WI* **FIELDS**, ISAAC *Pvt., Co. F, 14th WI* **FLICK**, C. B. *Pvt., Co. F, 11th WI* **FOOTE**, C. F. *Pvt., Co. I, 14th WI* **FOOTE**, JAMES *Pvt., Co. A, 52nd WI* **FRANKLIN**, BENJ. D. *Pvt., Co. K, 33rd WI* **FULLER**, HENRY *Pvt., Co. C, 3rd WI* **FULLER**, JOHN *Pvt., Co. H, 42nd WI* **GERGEN**, WM *Pvt., Co. H, 31st WI* **GILL**, JOHN *Pvt., Co. H, 58th PE* **GILLARD**, JAS. (a.k.a. HANDY, JAS.) *Pvt., Co., B, 1st WI Bat.* **GLASS**, L. J. *Pvt., Co. H, 61st IL* **GRAVES**, WILLIS *Pvt., Co. F, 19th U.S.* **GRAVES**, MICHAEL *Pvt., Co. D, 45th WI* **HAMILTON**, (HARRISON?) JESSE *Pvt., Co. M, 2nd NY* **HANKS**, ORIN *Pvt., Co. G, 32nd WI* **HARTSON**, E. G. *Pvt., Co. E, 41st WI* **HATCH**, JAMES *Pvt., Co. K, 38th WI* **HAYS**, SAM *Pvt., Co. A, 6th IL* **HIGGINS**, ERASTUS *Pvt., Co. C, 29th WI* **HILLYER**, FREDERICK *Pvt., Co. unassigned, 22nd WI* **HOAG**, JERRY *Pvt., Co. C, 28th NY* **HOLDEN**, E. M. *Pvt., Co. H, 48th WI* **HOLVERSON**, JOHN *Pvt., Co. B, 19th WI* **HUNTLEY**, WILLIAM *Pvt., Co. G, 51st WI* **JAMES**, ROBERT *Pvt., Co. E, 111th NY* **JOHNSON**, ENOCH B. *Pvt., Co. G, 2nd WI Cav.* **JONES**, JOHN B. *Pvt., Co. D, 12th WI and Co. C, 44th WI* **JONES**, G. H. *Pvt., Co. F, 164th NY* **KAPKA**, M. *2nd WI Bat.* **KEMERY**, JOHN *Pvt., Co. F, 27th NY* **KIMBALL**, JAMES A. *Pvt., Co. A, 29th WI* **KOPP**, JOSEPH *Pvt., Co. F, 16th IL* **LAVINE**, FRANK *Pvt., Co. E, 19th WI* **LESTER**, RICHARD *Pvt., Co. F, 7th WI* **LINDSAY**, FREEMAN D. *Pvt., Co. E, 118th NY* **LOWRY**, WM. H. *Pvt., Co. I, 42nd WI* **LUDINGTON**, GEO. A. *Pvt., Co. M, 30th OH* **McINTIRE**, IRA T. *Pvt., Co. A, 149th PE* **McVEAN**, JOHN *Pvt., Co. G, 20th WI* **MARKEY**, E. H. *Pvt., Co. I, 14th WI* **METCALF**, ANDREW *Pvt., Co. K, 144th OH* **MUMFORD**, JAS. R. *Pvt., Co. A, 52nd WI* **NEVERMAN**, WM. *Pvt., Co. I, 14th WI* **PALMER**, WM. *Pvt., Co. A, 6th WI* **PAULUS**, JOHN *Pvt., Co. M, 4th MO Cav.* **PAYSON**, WM. H. *Pvt., Co. G, 76th NY* **PHILLIPS**, G. N. *Pvt., Co. G, 23rd WI* **PIKE**, W. W. *Pvt., Co. I, 4th VT* **POPE**, JOHN *Pvt., Co. E, 113th IL* **POST**, M. M. *Pvt., Co. B, 2nd WI Cav.* **REDMOND**, GEO. *Pvt., Co. F, 20th ME* **REITZ**, FRED *Pvt., Co. I, 10th WI & Co. G, 21st WI* **ROBINSON**, CHAS. *Pvt., Co. F & C, 16th WI* **ROCKWELL**, HORACE *Pvt., Co. K, 10th WI* **ROGERS**, E. T. *Pvt., Co. C, 1st WI* **ROSE**, FRANCIS *Pvt., Co. E, 9th IL Cav* **RUNDLE**, FREDERICK *Pvt., Co. F, 124th NY* **SAFFORD**, D. L. *Hospital Steward, Co. ?, 174th & 27th OH* **SALSIBURY**, W. W. *Pvt., Co. I, 16th WI* **SCRANTON**, T. M. *Pvt., Co. A, 30th IA* **SHAVER**, AARON *Pvt., Co. G, 106th NY* **SHELDON**, G. G. *Pvt., Co. G, 42nd WI* **SHERMAN**, CHAS *Pvt., Co. F, 4th WI Cav.* **SHIELDS**, ALEX *Pvt., Co. B, 1st IA* **SILSBY**, J. E. *Cpl.., Co. D, 27th WI* SLATER, WM. *Pvt., Co. K, 30th IL* **SMITH**, AUGUSTUS

Pvt., Co. D, 12th WI **SONTAG**, LOUIS *Pvt., Co. D, 29th WI* **SOUTHARD**, A. B. *Pvt., Co. K, 11th ME* **SOUTHARD**, W. A. *Pvt., Co. K, 9th ME* **SQUIRES**, CHAS. *Pvt., Co. D, 14th WI* **STEVENS**, GEO. *Pvt., Co. A, 102nd NY* **STURDEVANT**, J. R. *Pvt., Co. I, 14th WI* **SUFFICOOL**, JOHN *Pvt., Co. B, 20th WI* **SWEETLAND**, GEO. *Pvt., Co. E, 1st NE Cav.* **TOLFORD**, J. W. *Pvt., Co. G, 23rd WI* **VERNAM**, DALLAS M. *Pvt., Co. E, 93rd NY & Co. H, 142nd* **WAGE**, FERNANDO C. *Pvt., Co. I, 14th WI* **WARDEN**, W. H. *Pvt., Co. K, 2nd, 36TH WI* **WEEKS**, LORENZO *Pvt., Co. A & C, 79th PE* **WEEKS**, STEPHEN *Pvt., Co. I, 17th WI & Co. H, 31st WI* **WELLS**, M. N. *Pvt., Co. ?, 7th WI Bat* **WHITE**, ALVIN *Pvt., Co. M, 1st NY Bat.* **WHITE**, GEORGE *Pvt., Co. A, 5th VT* **WIGHTMAN**, A. B. *Pvt., Co. A, 1st IL Lt. Art.* **WILSON**, GEO. M. *Pvt., Co. H, 3rd WI Cav. & Co. K, 54th WI* **WING**, ANDREW *Pvt., Co. G, 19th WI* **WOOD**, JOSEPH *Pvt., Co. E, 16th WI* **WOODWARD**, WM. F. *Pvt., Co. A, 64th NY* **WOODWORTH**, LUCIOUS *Pvt., Co. C, 49th WI* **YOUMANS**, H. J. *Pvt., Co. H, 23rd WI* **YOUNGLOVE**, MARTIN *Pvt., Co. ?, 34th MN*

Present day **TOWN OF SHERMAN** est. 1873
SPENCER (Marathon Co.) Post Office,

BOWMAN, EARL D. *Co. K, 39th WI* **CHARITON**, WM. *Co. A, 95th NY* **CLARK**, CALVIN L. *Sgt., Co. I, 1st WI* **FRAZIER**, JOHN H. *Sgt., Co. C, 108th IL* **GRIFFITH**, LEONARD *Co. C, 1st WI Cav.* **McPHERSON**, WM. B. *Co. E, 8th WI* **MARSH**, THOS. *Co. K, 110th NY* **MILES**, CHARLES C. *Co. E, 8th WI* **NEIL**, JAMES *Co. C, 39th MO* **PETERS**, ASHLEY *Co. L, 11th MO Cav.*
UPSON, JOSEPH B. *Cpl., Co. C, 1st WI Cav.* **VANDERHOOF**, WARD *Cpl., Co. C, 1st NJ* **VANDERHOOF**, WESLEY *Pvt., Co. E, 8th NJ* **WHIPPLE**, HENRY L. *Co. H, 18th WI*

BAY VIEW Post Office

MORGAN, DANIEL *Pvt., Co. B, 1st NJ Bat.*

Present day **TOWN OF SHERWOOD** est. 1874
NEVINS Post Office

BEATTY, G. S. *Pvt., Co. G, 50th NY* **GEISEN**, MATT *Pvt., Co. D, 28th NY* **JANES,** (Jones?) JOSEPH ALONZO *Cpl., Co. E, 7th WI* **LAFLESH**, THOMAS JEFFERSON *Captain, Co. B, 2nd WI Cav.* **PICKERING**, BYRON POTTER *Pvt., Co. A, 11th MI* **STOCKWELL**, CYRUS SIMEON *Surveyor, Co. F & S, 27th MI Inf*

Present day **TOWN OF THORP** est. 1876
THORP Post Office

ADAMS, J. *Pvt., Co. I, 61st PE* **BELLINGER**, PETER *Pvt., Co. G, 45th PE* **BIXBY**, WILLIAM *Pvt., Co. F, 9th VT* **BREED**, J. D. *Pvt., Co. B, 25th WI* **BROWN**, B. J. *Pvt., Co. G, 5th WI* **BURKHART**, CHRISTOPHER *Pvt., Co. E, 26th WI* **BUYALT**, WM. *Pvt., Co. G, 5th WI* **COLBY**, WM. *Pvt., Co. K, 25th WI* **DAILY**, W. H. *Sgt., Co. D, 24th MI* **FELLOWS**, VICTOR *Pvt., Co. D, 24th NY* **FERGUSON**, H. A. *Pvt., Co. E, 12th OH* **FIELDS**, O. H. *Pvt., Co. F, 1st MI* **FOSTER**, JEROME *Pvt., Co. D, 1st NY* **FRANCIS**, DANIEL S. *Pvt., Co. H, 2nd NH* **FREDEMAN**, CHRIST *Pvt., Co. D, 9th WI* **FULTS**, FRANK *(MN unknown unit)* **GLASSHOFF**, PETER *Pvt., Co. E, 21st WI* **HOWARD**, G. C. *Pvt., Co. H, 51st WI* **JERARD**, HENRY V. *Pvt., Co. G, 9th MI* **JERARD**,

WM. *Pvt., Co. F, 10th NY* **KELSER**, JOHN *Pvt., Co. B, 16th ME* **LAMPHERE**, ELISHA *Pvt., Co. B, 8th WI* **MABIE**, GEORGE *Pvt., Co. H, 31st WI* **MEAD**, V. R. *Pvt., Co. G, 49th WI* **NORTON**, JOHN *Pvt., Co E, 44th WI* **PHILLIPS**, R. W. *Pvt., Co. F, 48th WI* **PHILLIPS**, S. H. *Pvt., Co. D, 19th MI* **SCHMIDT**, GUSTAV *Sgt., Co. E, 27th WI* **SHERWOOD**, E. W. *Pvt., Co. D, 57th PE* **TIEDERMAN**, CHRIST *Pvt., Co. D, 9th WI* **TILDEN**, JAMES A. *Pvt., Co. A, 6th WI* **TOMPKINS**, H. H. *Pvt., Co. G, 3rd NY* **WARNER**, J.B. *Pvt., Co. F, 10th NY* **WARNER**, S. S. *Pvt., Co. F, 20th NY* **WORDEN**, ZEPHAMIAH *Pvt., Co. F, 45th PE*

Present day **TOWN OF UNITY** est. 1872
UNITY Post Office

BENNETT, JAMES *Pvt., Co. A, 169th NY* **BREMMISON**, JACOB *Pvt., Co. E, 130*[th] *OH* **BOWDEN**, J.C. *NonComOfficer, Co.C, 65*[th] *IL* **BROWN**, HENRY *Pvt., Co. G, 14th WI* **BROWN**, JOHN S. *Sgt., Co. H, 30th WI* **BROWN**, O. M. *Pvt., Co. M, 1st MI Cav.* **BURGESS**, C. H. *Pvt., Co. B, 4th WI* **DARTON**, A. E. *Pvt., Co. D, 45th WI* **DOERN**, CHRISTIAN *Pvt., Co. E, 21st NY* **EWALD**, KASE *Pvt., Co. D, 27th WI* **GARNETT**, JAMES *Pvt., Co. A, 2*[nd] *WI Cav.* **HARVEY**, J. P. *Sgt., Co. C, 21st WI* **HEALY**, C. *Pvt., Co. A, 2*[nd] *WI Cav.* **HENDERSON**, G. W. *Pvt., Co. M, 1st MN H. Art.* **HOW**, R. J. *Pvt., 10th NY Bat.* **HUBBARD**, W. J. *Pvt., Co. E, 74th IL* **JOHNSON**, J. N. *Pvt., 33rd NY Bat.* **KILTY**, WM. *Pvt., Co. F, 105th PE* **McHUGH**, A. *Pvt., Co. L, 7th WI* **PARKER**, JOHN *Pvt., Co. E, 96th NY* **PETTIT**, J. *Pvt., Co. B, 8th WI* **PICKETT**, S. H. *Pvt., Co. M, 1st WI Cav.* **POND**, W. D. *Sgt., Co. M, 4*[th] *MI Cav.* **RANDALL**, JAS. *Pvt., Co. B, 17*[th] *WI* **RANSOM**, N. *Cpl., Co. H, 47th WI* **ROOHR**, JACOB *Pvt., Co. D, 45th WI* **SCHOFIELD**, H. *Pvt., Co. K, 12th WI* **SHAFER**, SAMUEL *Pvt., Co. E, 52*[nd] *WI* **VAUGHAN**, D. B. *Cpl., Co. B, 118th NY* **YERKS**, OLIVER *Color Sgt., Co. K, 3rd NY*

Present day **TOWN OF WARNER** est. 1874
HEMLOCK Post Office

VARNEY, H. W. *Pvt., Co. A, 19th ME*

Present day **TOWN OF WASHBURN** est. 1873
SHORTVILLE Post Office

LOVELESS, SIMEON S. *Pvt., Co. M, 1st WI H. Art.* **ROBINSON**, GEO. *Cpl., Co. L, 2*[nd] *WI Cav.* **SHOOP**, ANDREW *Pvt., Co. F, 29th WI* **SHORT**, GEO. *Pvt., Co. D, 29th WI* **SHORT**, JAMES *Pvt., Co. D, 29th WI* **WINTERS**, J. M. *Pvt., Co. D, 29th WI*

Present day **TOWN OF WESTON** est. 1856
CHRISTIE Post Office

BARBER, J. L. *Pvt., Co. D, 16th WI* **BROWN**, SIDNEY *Sgt., Co. G, 3rd WI* **DIMOUTH**, JACOB *Pvt., Co. E, 21st WI* **GANDER**, L. V. *Pvt., Co. B, 3rd WI* **GATES**, CORTEZ *Pvt., Co. A, 4th WI* **KAYHART**, CHARLES *Pvt., Co. F, 27th NJ* **KETCHUM**, HUMPHREY *Pvt., Co. K, 9th IL* **MILLS**, CALVIN *Pvt. Co. E, 6th WI* **RANSOM**, SHERMAN *Pvt., Co. G, 14th WI* **ROBBINS**, JAS. W. *Pvt., Co. K, 1st OH* **ROSEMAN**, CHARLES *Pvt., Co. B, 19th WI* **SISCHO**, LEE *Pvt., Co. G, 14th WI* **SISCHO**, LUTHER *Pvt., Co. I, 38th WI* **SLATER**, GEORGE *Co. K, 39th IL* **TUTTLE**, ALBERT *Co. I, 38th WI* **WILCOX**, ISAAC *Pvt., Co. B, 16th NY* **WILSON**, REUBIN *Fife Major, Co. K, 24th NY*

Present day **TOWN OF WITHEE** est. 1880
STERLING Post Office

FESSENDEN, HENRY J. *Pvt., Band Leader, Co. D, 16ᵗʰ IL, Co. K, 18ᵗʰ IL*

Present day **TOWN OF YORK** est. 1873
WILCOX Post Office

BASSETT, EDWIN B. *Pvt., Co. A, 14th WI* **BENEDICT**, A. *Pvt., Co. A, 21st WI* **CURTIS**, ISRAEL *Pvt., Co. K, 4th U.S.H. Art. & Co. B, 9th OH Cav.* **LAWRENCE**, HORACE A. *Pvt., Co. E, 21st WI* **LINDSLEY**, GEORGE *Sgt., Co. A, 32ⁿᵈ WI* **PALMER**, Jos. L. *Pvt., Co. I, 1st WI* **PEASE**, SYLVESTER *Pvt., Co. H, 14th WI* **WILCOX**, SILAS A. *Lieut., Co. G, 10th WI*

Newspaper Clips

5 April 1888: **Charge Fargo** [Charles B. Fargo], of this city [Neillsville], an old soldier, and well known by all our people, died last Tuesday of pneumonia, after an illness of one week. He had been trying a long time to get a pension, and had just succeeded in finding his Captain, whose affidavit alone was needed to finish his case, and it is probable the claim would have been allowed within a week. But he has passed away, and whether his widow will be able to secure it remains to be seen. *The Clark Republican and Press (Charles served for the Union Army in the Civil War from 8 Sep 1864 - 30 May 1865)*

16 Aug 1894: Mrs. Hi Windover and Mrs. Huff went to Sheboygan County last week. **Mrs. Huff** has received $2000 back pension and $12 per month. *Republican and Press*

February 1907: Fred W. Draper reports a number of applications for an increase of pension already filed under the new act of Feb. 6, 1907; seven applications in the last five days. Under this law, Civil War veterans who served ninety days or more are entitled at 65 years of age, to $12 per month; at 70 to $15, and at 75 to $20. It will affect a great many old soldiers here. *Clark County Press*

December 1913: J. W. Tolford, who died at his home in Neillsville on Saturday morning, Dec. 20, 1913, was for many years one of the best known and most highly esteemed citizens of Clark County... Captain Tolford went out as lieutenant in the 23d WI, which was mustered into the service at Madison on Aug. 30, 1862. That regiment entered the service with 1,010 men. It was mustered out July 4, 1865, and there returned only 318 men and twenty-seven officers. The regiment traveled 11,000 miles, participated in fifteen engagements, and was under fire ninety-four days. A few years ago, Mr. Stockwell came to me and said that Captain Tolford was not drawing a pension that nearly all the old soldiers were getting pensions, but that the captain was too modest to apply. It was a surprise that one who so richly deserved his country's benefactions should not be receiving it. We went to our friend, obtained permission to act, and through Senator Spooner and Congressman Esch, secured the passage of a special act, giving the captain $30 a month. *Clark Co History 1918*

1903 Reunion at Neillsville, Clark Co, WI

Veterans with a Greenwood address: Joseph L. **Barber** Co D, 16 WI; H. W. **Barnett** Co E, 21 WI; John **Blecha** Co F, 34 WI; Jessie **Crane** Co B, 179 PA; John **Foust** Co H, 44 WI; Joe **Gibson** Co G, 12 WI; R. S. **Hummel** Co G, 10 & 5 WI; Charles **Roseman** Co B, 19 WI; Paul **Rossman** Co A, 9 WI; John **Tatro** Co E, 4 MN; Paschal **Wallis** Co K, 47 WI.

The hard-fighting 8th Wis. was often accompanied into battle by its mascot, Old Abe, a bald eagle which was a cherished bird. His care was assigned to two Madison soldiers, Q. M. Gen. McDonald and Capt. J. W. Tolford. The honor of carrying 'Old Abe' seated on his cannon perch was eagerly sought by many of the boys. John F. King of Neillsville was chosen as his special guard on one occasion when 'Old Abe' was transported to Clark County to take part in a reunion.

← Photograph of "Old Abe" by H. H. Bennett

November 1946

Three big days of celebration are planned for Clark County's returned soldiers, this coming weekend, beginning Saturday, November 9th. The **Civil War** will be represented, for instance, by the old flag which belonged to the G.A.R. post of Neillsville and which usually hangs in the W.R.C. hall. This G.A.R. flag was carried by a local unit in the Civil War. Also displayed will be the powder flask and an ink well owned by M. N. Wells, father of Burton Wells. M. N. Wells carried the flask and ink well during the Civil War. Another exhibit will be a framed clipping form a Vicksburg newspaper, together with a little piece of candy, upon which appears the legend, "Will you marry me?" **The candy was wrapped in a piece of newspaper by a little girl and given to George Meek**, the grandfather of W. B. Tufts, when the Federal troops entered Vicksburg. The Civil War exhibit is in charge of Burton Wells, who states that many trophies will be shown. *Clark County Press, Neillsville, WI "Good Old Days" November 14, 2001*

BIOGRAPHIES

Our information sources include birth, death, marriage, land and *VGR found at the Courthouse in Neillsville. We also purchased many military documents from the National Archives. Additionally, we made liberal use of newspaper microfilms held by the Wis. State Historical Society, Cemetery records, tombstone photos and area history books. These resources were combined with the research and photo albums contributed by family members. We cannot guarantee this work is error free, but we have done our very best to provide accuracy. We've included the Civil War Veterans we know resided in the townships of Beaver, Eaton, Warner and Weston who could have belonged to the John A. Eaton G.A.R. post #213 in 1885 until its closing in 1919. Those most actively engaged in this research were: Dick Adler, Lani Bartelt, Todd Braun, Linda Ewen, Paul Forster, Judy Hansen, Duane Horn, Marsha Hosfeld, Dolores Kenyon, Steven Lavey, Deb Sanger, Janet & Stan Schwarze, Sharon Short, Norma Telford, Crystal Wendt, Al Wessel, Ken Wood and Marla Zwakman.

"The majority of our information for Clark Co., Wis. Civil War Veterans came from the National Archives, Washington, DC. Many were awarded small pensions for their duty-related wounds or illnesses. Military and Pension records can contain an extensive history of the individual's specific situation that aren't included in this book: family details, examinations by physicians and statements from friends and neighbors. We encourage you to visit the Archives and avail yourselves of this informational treasure. I've found the Archives staff to be universally helpful and kind. Their website provides an excellent overview of their resources and what can be expected during research visits. I'd be pleased to provide specific guidance in this area." *Eidsvold native and Buff, Paul Forster, paul.forster@worldnet.att.net*

*VGR: L. A. Allen of Neillsville oversaw the veteran's graves registration work for the county and followed up the work even after the government called off the project before its completion. The Clark Co. Register of Deeds holds his work. Veterans buried in the county before 1938 were recorded. An example form is included in the first biography.

Franz "Frank" Friedrich ABEL 1845 – 1922 ☆
VGR#582, 18 Dec 1936, Next of kin: John Abel of Greenwood (son)

Frank was born in Mecklenburg, Germany, 27 Jan 1845. His parents, Henry and Maria Rasena (Bantin) Abel, came with their 8 children to the USA in 1857, first settling in Washington Co., WI. During the Civil War, Frank fought as a Pvt. with Co. F, 48th Wis. Inf.

VETERANS' GRAVES REGISTRATION

1. Veteran's Name ___Frank___ ___Abel___ 1a Serial No. _____
   First — Middle — Last — (If World War)

Last Address ___Greenwood, Wis.___

3. War in which veteran participated (check proper one): 3a Civil_X_ 3b Spanish___ 3c World___ 3d Other Wars___

4. Last Military Organization ___Co. F. 48 Wis. Inf.___ 4a Of Army_X_ Navy___ Others___

5. Date of Enlistment ___3/4/Oct 1865___ 5a Date Discharged ___2/13/1866___

6. Date of Death ___12/11/22___ 6a Rank ___Private___

7. Buried in ___Emmanuel Reformed___ Cemetery, 7a City of ___ or 7b Section No. 30, Township of ___Worden___

8. Grave No. -- 8a Lot No. 3 8b Block No. 1 8c Section --

9. Remarks ___ 9a Date of Birth ___1/27/34___

Veteran's next to kin ___Gustav Abel___ (Son) ___Greenwood, Wis. R. 2___
10a Relationship — 10b Address

11. Information furnished by ___John Abel___ (son) R 2 Greenwood, Wis. GAR Post, Greenwood, Wis.
(Relatives, Sexton of Cemetery, Post Records, etc.)

12. Character of present headstone or marker ___Priv. Stone Good___ 12a Is Government Headstone wanted? ___yes___

13. Data recorded by ___Harry T. Ketcham___ 13a County ___Clark___ 13b Date ___12/18/36___

Frank Abel's Veteran's Grave Registrations (VGR)

Frank served a year, being sent to western KS to watch over the Indians. Caroline Christine married him 22 Jan 1871 and for their first year together they lived with her parents. She was born 21 Oct 1852 in Washington Co., WI, the daughter of John and Sofia (Lutz) Dachler who located in Wayne Co. after emigrating from Germany. The young couple lived the next 2 years in Barton, WI and then moved in with his parents. After they died, Frank bought 80 acres of thick woodland in sec. 30, Warner Twp., Clark Co., WI in 1879. The road to it was merely a deer trail and it had no buildings on it. They brought with them enough supplies to last a year and began cultivating a farm with practically nothing but their callused hands. After a while they managed a team of oxen and later one of steers, which Frank broke himself. The log cabin they built was 18 x 24 feet and they called it home for 25 years before building a new frame home. They also built a log barn and during their first summer they got a cow from Mr. Baker. As the years rolled by and the trees were stumped, a modern farm with frame buildings and 60 cleared acres replaced the former forest bed. The Abels had 6 children. Wilhelm "Will" Friedrich (29 Feb 1872), Franz "Frank" Johannas (1 Jan 1874, West Bend, WI) and Friedrich "Fred" (2 Oct 1878, d. 12 Feb 1902) accompanied them to Clark Co., WI. Fred was killed on the railroad after his 24th birthday. The 3 others: Johannes "John" Heinrich (6 Oct 1882), Gustav "Gus" Heinrich (15 Oct 1885) and Hulda Karoline (11 Oct 1891, d. 29 Mar 1903) were born on their farm in sec. 30, Warner Twp., near the lost community of Thielen. Frank served as school board director and helped build the Reformed Church, where he was both an officer and janitor. Caroline and Frank celebrated their last Christmas together in 1921. She passed away 7 Mar 1922 he died 11 Dec 1922. Both of were buried in the UCC East Cemetery next to the farm where they lived for so many years.

"A healthy girl was born to Mr. and Mrs. Frank Abel on the West Side Sunday evening." *Greenwood Gleaner, 5 Aug 1909--10 yrs ago, granddaughter of Frank & Caroline.*

William George AUSTIN 1837 – 1919

1885 Special WI Veterans' Census, Greenwood Residence

William was born 1 Nov 1837 in Herkimer, Washington Co., NY. In 1854 he moved to Wisconsin with his parents, Palmer and Catherine (Peckham) Austin, where they "improved" the first farm in the La Crosse Valley. Mary "Sarah" Emeline Fosdick, the daughter of Lyman and Betsy Fosdick, married William 4 Mar 1857 in Kenosha where her family had settled in 1842.

← **William Austin & Family**

30

The Austin's first two daughters were born in Sparta: Ida Blanche (2 Jan 1858), and Catharine Marie (27 Nov 1859). Their only son, William Irving (28 Feb 1862), was born in Little Falls. The following year "Sarah" was left to care for these children without her husband when he enlisted with Co. C, 19th Wis. Inf. in Madison, WI, 8 Dec 1863. Pvt. Austin had blue eyes, brown hair, a light complexion and stood 5'11" tall. After serving on provost duty at Fredericksburg and Warrenton, VA, he was mustered out 9 Aug 1865 at Richmond, VA, and returned to his family in Sparta. F. C. Brooks taught him the lucrative art of barrel making. Because all sorts of foods could be stored in these containers, a cooper such as William was assured a reliable income. Sauerkraut could be fermented in such casks and they were an ideal way to transport flour, gunpowder, tobacco, dried and salted fish or meat. Fragile items such as eggs could be packed in them among layers of straw to keep them cooler and they were invaluable for storing liquids from wine to milk. Three more children joined their family: Vinona Ellen (24 Jan 1864), Alma Edith (2 Apr 1867) and Sarah Jane "Jennie" (7 Nov 1868). They moved to Galesville right after Jennie was born and just after the calendar was turned to 1870, William became a foreman in the cooper's shop for Wilson Davis' new flour mill. While living in Galesville William served as an officer and "District Deputy" in the I.O.O.F that was organized 30 Oct 1874. Over ten years later, the Austins moved to Greenwood in the heart of Clark Co., Wis. and Jennie married Geo. B. M. Warner, 31 Dec. 1884. Alma also married one of the local boys, Louis B. Cook, 24 Oct 1885. Vinona married Virgil W. Hatch in Bangor, SD, 25 Sep 1888. By 1900, the Austins were living in Mabton, Yakima, WA where William died 16 Jun 1919 and was buried in the local cemetery, lot 71, grave 2.

*Benjamin Franklin Chase, John Holverson, **Frank Lavine**, **Charles Roseman** and **Andrew Wing** also fought with the 19th Wis. and lived in Clark Co., WI.

Moses BABB 1824-1895 ☆🏳

VGR #157, dated 27 Feb 1937, Next of Kin: Don Warner, Greenwood, WI (Grandson)

Moses was born 3 Jan 1824 in Gardiner, Kennebec, ME. His ancestors have been traced to the earliest days of America. He was the son of Joseph Babb (son of Joshua[7], Joshua[6], Joshua[5], Phillip[4], Phillip[3], Phillip[2], Thomas[1]) who married Margaret Davis. Louisa Prissey (1837) was eighteen when she became Moses' bride in Racine Co., WI, 24 Sept 1855. They lived in the village of Caledonia, where Moses kept the bread on their table with his blacksmithing skills, and later moved to Mt. Pleasant. With an anvil and a hammer, Moses could forge things from his iron and use them as currency to trade or barter for virtually anything his family might need including flour from the mill, a good horse, or medicine.

With an anvil and a hammer, Moses could forge things from his iron and use them as currency to trade or barter for virtually anything his family might need including flour from the mill, a good horse, or medicine. His shop was the heart of the community because he could make the tools needed for other trades. But when the Civil War broke out, Moses left his business to become a soldier. He said his good-byes to Louisa and his young son, Eugene

(1857 ca) and marched off to war with the 20th Wis. Inf., 12 Feb 1864. He transferred to Co. C, 35th Wis. Inf., 2 July 1865 before being discharged with a disability, 18 Jan 1866. His younger brother, Joseph Jr., fought with Co. D, 7th ME Inf. Moses married a second time, 14 Mar 1870. His bride was Mary Ann (Weber) Hommell who was born in Württemberg, Germany 13 Aug 1825 and had come to America in 1849. She was the widow of John M. Hommell and the mother of 5 children: John William "Tom", Charles Henry, Mary (m. Leroy Weber, 16 Dec 1882), George and Edward. The Babb's home was known as "The Drake place" and it stood near the road on the west side of the Black River in sec. 34, Warner Twp, Greenwood, WI. During 1887, rising flood waters threatened to destroy it, but by the grace of God, the surge stopped at the edge of their porch. Their closest neighbor was George A. Austin, the foreman of the Michaeljohn and Hatton stavemill, who lived across the road near the gravel pit. Eugene Babb worked in the logging camps. Moses passed away 2 Jun 1895 and was buried in the Greenwood, WI City Cemetery. Eugene died a month later, 7 Jul 1895 and was buried in the Poor Farm Cemetery in York Twp. Mary Ann's life ended 22 Jan 1913 and she was buried next to Moses.

Joseph Lanning BARBER, Sr. 1827 - 1904
VGR #525, dated 15 Jul 1937

Joseph was born 10 Oct 1827 in NJ, the son of a shoemaker, John S. and his wife, Abigail (Kinneman) Barber. His Hessian father came to the USA to fight against Americans in the Revolutionary War, but deserted by jumping off a man-of-war to swim ashore, joining Washington's army and serving as an officer until the end of that war. In 1847, Jacob went to Chemung Co., NY, where that summer, he married Frances E., the daughter of John and Hannah M. Demouth. At the age of 22 years, he learned the ship-carpenter's trade. In 1851, this young couple moved to Calumet Co., WI, going first to Holstein, and finally settling on an 80 acre farm in Hayton. They raised a family of 7 children. At one time or another, Joseph held most of the town offices, serving as Town Clerk for 8 years and District Clerk for 18 years. He was a member of both the Masons and the I.O.O.F. During the Civil War, Jacob enlisted 6 Sep 1864 as a Pvt. with Co. D, 16th Wis. Inf. He served a year and fought in the battles of Savannah, Fort McAllister and others, before being honorably discharged 2 Jun 1865. When he died, 10 Sep 1904, of Bright's disease and heart failure, he was buried in the East Weston Cemetery, now known as Chapel Hill.

"J. L. Barber has carpenters at work building a new house." *The Republican and Press, 18 Aug 1887*

Stillman H. BENJAMIN 1837 - 1910 ☆ ⚑

Stillman was born 26 Nov 1837*, the son of Isaac Stillman and Rachel (Annis) Benjamin in Moscow, Somerset Co, Maine. His ancestors were colonists from England and his grandfather, Abezer Benjamin, reportedly entered the American Revolution as a drummer at the age of 17. Stillman and his wife Sarah, the daughter of Stephen and Almira Dunbar, married 12 Dec 1862 in Wautoma, Waushara Co., WI. She was born 3 Sep 1843 in NY. The following year Stillman enlisted as a Pvt. with Co. G, 32nd and Co. D, 16th Wis. Inf. and was honorably discharged 4 Jul 1865. His brothers Cyrus (1830), Sylvester (11 Nov 1831) and Ephraim** (1840) also served for the Union. After the war Stillman and Sarah farmed in

Omro, Winnebago Co., WI. Three of the Benjamin's children who were born there: William G. (Apr 1866, m. Ida May Goodwin); Orin "Orrie" Albert (1866); Arvilla (1868, m. Oscar Orr). Shortly thereafter they began farming in Bennington, Mower Co., MN where Stillman Jr. (1870, MN, m. Flora McKee) was born. They later moved to Hamilton, Spring Valley, MN which was only a few miles from Stillman's parents, brother Cyrus, and other family members. Alfred (Sept 1877, MN, m. Jessie Skyhawk); Clara "Carrie" Belle (1879, MN, m. C. T. Conlon); and Cora "Sarah" Laura (Dec 1882, m. McHenry) were born there. Family records indicate the Benjamins moved to ND, but they apparently returned to Spring Valley, MN where they were farming when both the 1900 and 1910 census were taken. In 1903, William G. and Ida bought the Morris Markham farm in Sec. 17, Warner Twp. Clark Co., WI. Their land was next to what was once known as the "Schwarze School" and later became known as the "Benjamin School." Stillman grew ill in 1910 and he moved to Clark County just before the oats were ready for threshing to stay with William and Ida May. He died in their home 19 Sep 1910 and was buried in the Greenwood, WI City Cemetery. He had a fine moral character, sturdy constitution, and was a faithful member of the Wesleyan Methodist Church. We believe Sarah moved to Omro, WI to be near her extended family and died there, 20 Aug 1927.

*200 yr. old family Bible says 2 Jun 1837, but census records & obituary indicate a Nov birth date.
Ephraim Benjamin and **Joseph Lanning Barber also fought with Co. D, 16th Wis. Inf.

Freeman Silas BLANCHARD 1840 - 1927
1885 Special Veterans Index, Weston, Clark Co. WI

Freeman was born in 26 Aug 1840 in Washington, Sullivan Co., NH, the son of Silas and Martha J. (Smith) Blanchard. In 1860 he was working there as blacksmith. While residing in Sutton, NH, he married Hannah Greely Keyser, 16 Aug 1862 in Sutton just a day after he'd joined the Union Army. He fought as a Pvt. with Co. F, 11th NH during the Civil War, but deserted his company, 13 Nov 1862 at Sulphur Springs, VA. Hannah was born 30 Nov 1846 in Sutton, Merrimack Co., NH, the daughter of Simon and Mary Ann (Pinney) Kezar. The children of Freeman and Hannah were: Mary J. (1865, Canada), Walter M. (1867, NH), Leon (1869, NH), Eda S. (Jul 1871), William C. (Nov 1873), James F. (Jan 1876), Frederick Harvey (17 Jan 1878), Tina Maud (Feb 1880, WI) and Ada Bell (Sep 1882). The Blanchards Farmed in Weston Twp., Clark Co. WI. Hannah passed away, 29 Nov 1913 in Jefferson, Linn Co., OR and Freeman died 1 Apr 1927 in Philomath, Benton Co., Oregon.

Jan Nepomuk "John" BLECHA 1839 - 1926
Assumed Member of John A. Eaton G.A.R. post #213

"John" was born in Skoric, Bohemia, Czechoslovakia, 4 Jul 1839, the son of Frantisek and Jozefa (Bilek) Blecha. At age 17, he moved to Washington Co., WI with his parents, 3 sisters and 3 brothers, arriving at the New Orleans port in 1857. Five years later, John enlisted with Co. B, 34th Wis., Inf., 20 Dec. 1862, at Milwaukee for Civil War service. Pvt. Blecha was 5'8' tall, had blue eyes and brown hair. The following year he was appointed Cpl., 1 Jan 1863 and Musician in the Drum & Bugle Corp., 24 Feb 1863. He was discharged 8 Sep 1863 at Milwaukee, WI as a sick man. His doctor recommended he be given a half-disability pension because he suffered with diarrhea, bad lungs, rheumatism and neuralgia.

At the time of his death he was receiving $65 a month. Anna became his bride, Nov. 10, 1875, in Newburg, WI. She was born in Bohemia, Czechoslovakia, 21 Apr 1852, the daughter of Franz "Frank" and Katherine "Katie" (Smertina) Klinka.

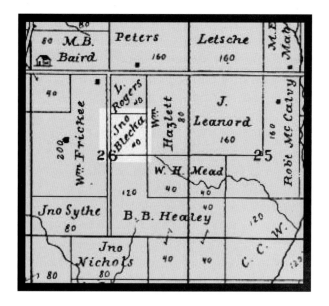

The Blechas had 4 children: James John (16 Sep 1876) of Beloit, WI; Frank Joseph (7 Apr 1878), Mary Anna (13 Mar 1881, m. Wm. H. Kubat of Granton), WI, and Anna B. (13 Oct 1885). John Blecha was a resident of Clark Co. WI, for over 40 years. The family farm was in sec. 26 of Eaton Twp., on the "26 road".

←**Blecha Farm, sec. 26, Eaton Twp**

*The biographies of **W. H. Mead** & **Robt. McCalvy** are also included in this book.

John was struck with the infirmities of old age, but they never totally blocked his every ready smile. Anna lost a battle with cancer, at midnight just before Christmas, 18 Dec 1900 and was buried 3 days later in St. Anthony's Cemetery, Loyal, WI. John's last day arrived 2 Nov 1926, after two months of intense suffering at the home of his daughter, Anna (m. Frank White of Chattaroy, WA). His body was shipped back to Loyal, WI, where a funeral was held at St. Balthazar's Church followed by his burial in the Catholic Cemetery.

John H. BOOTH 1839 – 1919 ☆ ⌒

VGR#158, Next of kin: Alta B. Hartson (g-daughter) of San Francisco, CA, Infor: H. H. Hartson & John Arends

John Booth

John H. Booth

John was born 22 Dec 1839 at Rhinebeck, NY. Angeline C. "Angie" became his wife 5 Jul 1861. She was born 25 Apr 1842 in Oswego, NY, the daughter of Lewis and Julia (De Rosa) Fertile. As a little girl, she moved with her parents to Rockford, IL, before settling Rochester, MN, a few years later. The Booths were pioneer settlers on the prairie of Brookfield, MN, where they raised their children: Frances (1863), Nellie Irene (1 Sep 1864, Rochester, MN, m. Wm. Palms), Charles (1867), Vern Louis (1870), Luella (1876) and Florence (1880). John fought as a private in the Civil War with Co. H, 11th MN, Inf. He enlisted 29 August 1864 and was discharged 26 June 1865.

Just before Christmas in 1895, they sold their farm and moved to Greenwood, WI, and then built a home on Andrews Ave. in 1900. In 1910 John became the first Greenwood Cemetery Sexton. Everyone seemed to know this likable man. For many years, his name was published weekly in the local paper, the *Greenwood Gleaner,* because he was the Commander of John A. Eaton Post #213. When Angie died 26 Feb 1912, **Rev. S. E. Sweet** of the Baptist church conducted the service and **William Oelig**, **John Blecha**, **Charles Wollenberg** and **Pascal Wallis** were pall bearers. She was buried in the Greenwood City Cemetery. John died 5 years later, 13 Jan 1919 and is resting beside her.

Jacob BRENEMAN 1843 - 1919
1895 Special WI Veterans Census

"Jake" was born in Ohio during Feb 1842, the son of John and Jane (Wiman) Breneman. He married Mary M., 30 Dec 1869. She was born 20 Jul 1852, the daughter of David S. and Maryette (Barker) Clark. Jacob and Mary farmed in sec. 3, Beaver Twp, Clark Co. WI. They were the parents of three sons: Eugene B., Wesley and Elmer, and a daughter, Mary Cora. Jacob was a veteran of the Civil War, having fought as a Pvt. with Co E, 130th OH Inf. for 1 yr., 4 mos. He enlisted at Toledo, 2 Mar 1864 and was discharged 2 Jul, 1865. At the time of the 1870 Census, Jacob's mother was residing with the family, but in 1880, she was living with Jacob's brother, Henry, in Poynette, WI. Apparently the rigors of war and life took a heavy toll on Jake because family members described him as a rather cantankerous individual who was not always kind to his wife. He died 7 Apr 1919 and was interred in Clark Co., but after Mary passed away in 1935, his remains were moved to the Marcellon Cemetery at Pardeeville, and buried next to her.

Hiram N. BRINTNALL 1842 – 1910
VGR #11, dated 11 Mar 1937, Next of kin: Mrs. GEO. Bowen of Montesano, WA (daughter)

Hiram W. Brintnall was born 16 Apr 1834 in Northumberland, Canada, to a father who was a native of NY and an Irish mother. Christmas Day, 1858, he and Amelia S. (Dec 1840, NY) were married. She was the daughter of Chapen and Eliza Ann (Ackerman) Warner. The Brintnalls were living in Kewaskum, Washington Co., WI in 1860 and were the parents of 8 month old Herbert James (1859, m. "Minnie" Tiedemann). Two years later duty called and Hiram enlisted as a Pvt. with Co. E, 27th Wis. Inf., 21 Aug 1862 and was later transferred to Co. I. He was promoted to Full Sgt. before being mustered out 29 Aug 1865. He'd participated in the Siege of Vicksburg, the capture of Little Rock, and the evacuation of Camden. His family had expanded while he was on the battlefield and his return home meant he could hold Jane Eliza "Jennie" (1863, m. George Bowen) for the first time. Five years later, Nellie S. (1868, m. Freeman Clark), arrived. Harriet R. "Hattie" (1870, m. Frank Godfrey) came along and by then they were living in Loyal, WI, where Robert A. (1873) was also born. The rigors of war and the responsibilities of his growing family must have taken a significant toll on Hiram as he spent some time in both the Mendota and Wausau hospitals for mental issues. A homestead record dated 25 Apr 1877 shows he acquired 98 acres in sec. 6 & 7, Unity Twp. Their youngest, Luretta A. (15 Aug 1880, m. John Herman Vogt) was born there. Jennie, Hattie and Luretta all taught school in the county and Herbert may have done local photography. Hiram passed away 1 Jul 1910 and was laid to rest in Beaver Twp.

Cemetery. Several of the children located in WA, and Amelia filed for her widow's pension there in Aug 1910. She died 17 Sep 1913 in Seattle, WA.

*Fred Buker, George Wesley Courter, George Kesler, **Henry Decker** and Joseph E. Silsbey all lived in Clark Co., WI, and also fought with the 27th Wis. and served at the same time.

Benjamin Franklin "Frank" BROWN 1844 – 1919 ☆

"Frank" was born 23 Mar 1844 in Marengo, McHenry, IL, the son of Peris and Achsah (Hart) Brown who were natives of VT. After moving to an Illinois farm in 1842, they opened a mercantile business in Huntley Grove. In 1856 they opened a new store in Black River Falls, WI and lived there for 8 years before moving to their last home in Augusta, Eau Claire, WI. A veteran of the Civil War, Frank served as 1st Sgt. with Co. G, 5th Wis. Inf. along with his brother, Bernard of Thorp. After mustering in at Madison, they joined Gen. Grant's Army of the Potomac and participated in the battles of Petersburg, Sailor's Creek, Richmond and others, being present at the fall of Richmond, and at Lee's surrender at Appomattox.

Following the Grand Review* at Washington, D. C., they returned to Jackson Co., WI. In 1869 Frank married Nancy Jeanette "Nettie" (1 Feb 1850 WI), the daughter of James and Harriet M. (Woodworth) Chandler, who both began their life in NY. The Chandlers had opened the first grocery store in Black River Falls in 1846. Nettie's brother **Woody Chandler** had served with Frank and Bernard during the Civil War. Their sister, Ann Emmeline Brown, married **Alfred S. Eaton** who later became a founding member of the John A. Eaton GAR Post. In 1870 the Chandlers sold out and moved to Eaton Twp., Clark County, with their daughter and new son-in-law. They opened the *Brown and Chandler General Store* in a rented building owned by Steven Case Honeywell. The following year, the Chandlers returned to Black River Falls, selling their interests in the partnership to Elijah Barton Brown of Pine Valley who was later convicted of killing Fred Drake of Hewett. After the village was platted in 1871, Frank Brown had a new store built on the second block of School St. He also became the first postmaster. That same year Nettie gave birth to their daughter, Maude B.–the first white child born in the newly named town, *Greenwood*. She died about 13 years later and was buried in Augusta, WI. After Frank and Nettie moved to MN, the Arend Bros. business replaced their store. Frank had been retired from the Lumber business for 20 years when he died at age 75 of throat cancer on 17 Jun 1919. He passed away in his home at 1808 Irving Ave. S., Minneapolis, MN at 2 p.m. After Frank's death, Nettie lived at 3527 Aldridge Ave., Minneapolis. At age 89, she died at the Deaconess Hospital on 2 Nov 1936. They are both buried in the Lakewood Cemetery.

* (see page 120)

Sidney BROWN 1835 - 1912
VGR #526, dated 15 Mar 1937

Sidney was born in St. Lawrence Co., NY, 2 Jul 1835, the son of Benjamin Carr and Lucy Brown. He married Lydia, the daughter of Hirum and Lucinda (Eldridge) Harlow, 2 Oct 1857. She was born 2 Oct 1837 in VT and raised in Oswegatchie, NY. Shortly before the outbreak of the Civil War and their move to Brown Co., WI, the Browns buried their infant son, Clarence. Sidney enlisted as a Pvt. in the 3rd Wis. Cav. and served gallantly through the war and mustered out as a Q. M. Sgt. Following his return to civilian life, he tackled the task of clearing a new farm near Wrightstown, WI. About 1876 he claimed a homestead in Summit, KS. When they moved to Clark County in 1881, they purchased a farm 2 miles east of the Christie post office. They later sold it and moved to another Christie farm, which was ultimately Sidney's last home. They were the parents of 6 children: Clarence (1859 ca., d. NY), Sarah L. (1858), Alta (1861), Elmer (Nov 1866), Albia Carr (30 Nov 1868, d. 1 Jan 1943, Portland OR) and Lillian "Lillie" (1874, m. Edgar Sischo). Lydia died 11 Feb 1890 and was buried in the Weston Chapel Hill Cemetery. Six years later, Maria Simons of Kaukauna, WI, became Sidney's 2nd wife, 25 May 1896. She was born Jul 1851 in Calumet Co., WI, the daughter of James and Martha (Skeesuck) Simons. Sidney was a strong, forceful man. As lumber camp foreman, a pioneer on the forest farm or western prairie, a soldier in the field, a leader in local political affairs, as a citizen or neighbor, he constantly strived to unite and build. He became one of the most respected citizens of the area. As a carpenter his skilled hands framed many of the buildings around the county and like Sidney, they were strong and stable. He died 1 Mar 1912 and is buried near Lydia. When Maria died 9 Aug 1935, she too was laid to rest there.

Friedrich Harmon Conrad BUKER 1840 - 1924 ☆
VGR #583, dated 13 Jan 1937; Next of kin: Edward Buker (son) of Greenwood, WI

"Fred" was born in Lippe Detmold, Germany, 13 Sep 1840, the son of Harmon and Caroline (Reineking) Buker. At the age of 7, he came with his parents to the USA. His sister, Catherine, died on the voyage and was buried at sea. They settled on 160 acres of woodland in Herman Twp., Sheboygan Co., WI along with 16 other families. Fred was 21 years old when the Civil War broke out in 1861. That following summer, 21 Aug 1862, he enlisted with Co. C, 27th Wis. Inf. Volunteers and served three years before his discharge as a corporal, 29 Aug 1865.

←The original 11 X 14" charcoal drawing of Fred Buker in Military Dress, pictured here, is now in the possession of his great grandson, Owen Haigh, Neillsville, WI.

Being a good shot, he was often called upon to do scout duty, the colonel of the regiment attaching him to his person in confidential capacity for special service. His marksmanship was afterwards often demonstrated in Clark County at turkey and goose "shoots," and gave him fame throughout the county. He served in every battle in which his regiment took part, and came out of the war without a scratch indeed; it was a favorite joke in his company that he could not be killed. After the war Fred farmed on his father's place until 1873, and then made an overland journey by wagon to Neillsville, WI, hauling 2,700 pounds in freight to homestead land in sec. 24 of Warner Twp. His wife, the former Charlotte Schaper who he had married Dec 1865, later arrived by train accompanied by their sons Fred and Edwin. George, another son, was born in Clark County. Fred had to cut his own road to the site where an existing old log building stood waiting to house this brave pioneer family. Fred soon erected a new cabin and in the 2nd year, built a log barn, 32' x 72'. A couple of years later he purchased woodland in sec. 19 that could only be reached by a trail. With his own hands, Fred cleared 130 acres in 8 years, while simultaneously lumbering in the woods during the winter. He built a fine, large house and one of the first basement barns in the area, but in 1904 it was struck by lightning and burned to the ground, with the loss of a bull and 1,000 bushels of oats and 100 tons of hay. Had it happened a few moments later, all of his milk cows would also have been inside. Though it rained in torrents in many places that evening, hardly a drop fell on his property. Charlotte died 5 Feb 1909, and Fred died at the ripe old age of 84 yrs, 29 Oct 1924. They were buried on the West Side of the Black River in Warner Twp., in the Evangelical & Reformed Cemetery. Fred was one of the founding members of that church, helped to build it and worshiped there for many years.

"Fred Buker, of the Town of Hixon, received back pension through Clerk of Court Parkhurst a few days ago. The pension amounted to $1,086, being allowed $6 per mo." *Rep. & Press, Oct 1880*

Andrew James BULLARD 1842 – 1926 ca.
1885 Special WI Veterans' Census, Neillsville

Andrew J Bullard

Andrew farmed and raised stock in sec. 24, Weston Twp. He was born in Menominee, WI, 16 Jun 1842. His father, Sanford Bullard, a millwright, was one of the earliest settlers of Milwaukee. His mother Martha Gasser, a native of Switzerland, arrived in America at the age of eight. Her father had died aboard ship during their voyage, but the fatherless family went on to settle in OH. Andrew was 19 years old when he enlisted as a Pvt. with the Union Army, 17 Sep 1861. He was taller than the average soldier of the times, standing 5'11". His eyes were blue and he had a light complexion with auburn hair. He served 4 years with Co. D, 12th Wis. Inf., engaging in the sieges of Vicksburg, Jackson, and Atlanta, and was with Sherman in the grand march to the sea. The majority of the time he was a Cpl. and was discharged 12 Jun 1862. His brother **Geo. W. Bullard** also served. After the war he farmed in Boltonville., WI. Rev. Charles Woodward joined Andrew and Harriet Rowena Verbeck (1847) in marriage at their friend's home 24 Feb 1867. She was born in West Bend and was the daughter of Joseph H. and Elizabeth (Carter) Verbeck. The Bullards had 3 sons: Merton A. (3 Jan 1868), Rueben R. (21 Sep 1872, m. Mattie Shaw), Bertram "Bert" M. (14 Apr 1875); and 3 daughters, Seula "Lula" J. (1 Jun 1877), Martha "Mattie" E. (25 Jul 1880, d. 13 Oct 1891) and Iva J. (25 May 1885). In the autumn of 1870, they entered a claim to a tract of heavy timberland in Clark County. In the spring of 1871, he erected a pole shanty and in the fall built a log house. That winter he worked in the pineries. The next spring they gained full ownership of their farm and began raising Holstein and short-horn cattle. Andrew was elected Clerk of the School Board, Trustee of his School District, County Supervisor, and the agent and director of the Lynn Insurance Company. He voted a Republican ticket. Harriet died 15 Nov 1891, 3rd in her family to be taken to the grave by Typhoid Fever that fall. She was buried beside Lulu and, "Mattie" in the Weston West Cemetery, Clark Co. WI. Adelia Elizabeth became his 2nd wife, 15 Nov 1893. She was the daughter of **Robert and Anna (Rector) McCalvy**. She'd first married another Civil War veteran, Albert S. Gray, 15 May 1868 and later George E. Castner (3 Jul 1882, Neillsville, WI) but they'd divorced Oct 1893. In 1888 Andrew applied for a military pension in Neillsville, WI, and asked for reinstatement after moving to Santa Rosa, Sonoma Co., CA. Adelia died Jun 1915 in Santa Rosa, CA and Andrew died ca. 1926. They are both buried in the Santa Rosa Rural Cemetery (707) 542-1580.

"A. J. Bullard hiced (hived) a swarm of bees August 3rd and Aug. 23rd, the bees made 75 lbs of honey." *Clark Co., Press, 1895.*

George Washington BULLARD 1844 - 1917
1885 Special WI Veterans' Census, Neillsville

George was born 26 Feb 1844 in Milwaukee, WI, to Sanford (1801) and Martha Bullard (1820 ca.). His father was born in Vermont and his mother was a native of Switzerland. His father purchased a farm in Washington Co., 1 Sep 1848 at the Milwaukee Land Office. George's siblings were: **Andrew J.**, who was a year older than George, Reuben R. who was 3 years younger; and Warren C. who was six years younger. George fought as a private with Co. E, 27th Wis. Inf. during the Great Civil War. This regiment was largely composed of German Immigrants. George's brothers Andrew and Reuben also served for the Union Army. George was living in Farmington, Washington Co. WI at the time of his enlistment, 21 Aug 1862. **Hiram Brintnall** of Beaver Twp. fought with this same company and enlisted the same day. **Henry Decker** signed on to that same regiment the next day and **Fred Buker** joined it the following week. George was on duty at Young's Point, Snyder Bluff and Haines' Bluff, LA. He also participated in the Siege of Vicksburg, MS; the capture of Little Rock, AR; the campaign against Mobile, AL; the siege of both Fort Blakely and Spanish Fort and many others. Because these soldiers were so often sent to the swamps and trenches in those southern states, more lives were lost to malaria, scurvy, malnutrition and dysentery than on the battlefield. George was mustered out 29 Aug 1865 at Brownsville, TX. Five years later Emily Charisey, the daughter of Joseph H. and Elizabeth (Carter) Verbeck, became his bride on 9 Jan 1870. Their wedding took place in West Bend, Washington, WI. Their children were: Nellie Arlette (21 Oct 1878 in Neillsville), Ora Earl (5 Mar 1875 in Neillsville), Rupert George (7 Mar 1871 in Oakfield, Fond du Lac, WI) and Emogene Whitney (21 May 1873 in Neillsville). The 1880 Federal Census shows this family lived in Weston Twp., Clark Co. WI, and George was issued a homestead 10 Apr 1882 at the Eau Claire land office for sec. 4 of Weston West in what is today known as Seif Twp. About 1897 the family moved to Chetek where Emily passed away 22 Jun 1917. On 6 Jul 1917, George died at St. Joseph's Hospital following an operation. Both were buried in the Forest Hill Cemetery in Chippewa Falls, WI.

Chester Hamilton BURGESS 1827 - 1919

1885 Special WI Veterans' Census

Chester was born Christmas Day in Boonville, NY, in 1827. At the age of 20 yrs, he went to Mendon, NY, to farm and work on the Erie Canal. He became the husband of Amy Lunt, 1 Jan 1850. She was born in NY, on Christmas Day, 1831--*exactly* 4 years separating their ages. In 1853 they purchased a farm in Fond du Lac Co., WI. Nine years later, Chester enlisted in Co. B, 4th Wis. Cav., becoming color bearer and serving with distinction until returning to Fond du Lac Co. with an honorable discharge. He immediately moved to IA, but returned to Fond du Lac just 2 years later. During June 1870 they moved to Clark Co., WI, making an overland journey with a horse team to homestead 160 acres of wild, heavily timbered land in sec. 1, Beaver Twp. They built a log shanty with a bark roof and "puncheon floor", which are logs split in half and tightly laid split side-up. This made for a warm floor,

Chester & Amy (Lunt) Burgess

snugly fitting to the sides and end of the building. There were no mop boards to give a smooth finish. Clearing the land was an arduous task spanning many years but eventually a well-developed, profitable farm, new house, barn and outbuildings took shape. The first town meeting for Beaver Twp. was held at the Burgess home the first Tuesday in April 1871. Chester was elected chairman and represented that board as a county commissioner. Chester and Amy had four children: Harriet Ann (15 Oct 1851) and Rosetta (3 Nov 1855) each died at the age of eighteen; Mary Luvina (21 Oct 1853) was married the 4th of July 1871, in her father's log cabin in Beaver Twp., to Edward Bowen. George Burgess (3 Mar 1871) married Clara Britten. The Burgess family attended the Methodist Episcopal Church. In 1913 they sold their farm and retired in the village of Unity. Two years later, Chester died at the age of eighty-seven, 13 Jan 1915, while staying at the home of his daughter, Mary Bowen, in Marshfield. Amy lived to have the distinction of being mother, grandmother, great-grandmother and great-great-grandmother. She was also a member of the Rebekah Lodge. Amy applied for her widow's pension 8 Feb 1915. Chester, Amy, Rosetta and Harriet were laid to rest in the Brighton Cemetery, Marathon Co., WI.

Joseph BUTTERFIELD 1826 - 1897
1895 Special WI Veterans' Census

Joseph was born 27 Nov 1826 in ME, the son of John Butterfield (1781 ca.) who was born in NH and lived in Hartland, ME. John Jr. (1823), Hiram (1829) and Mary (1830) were his siblings. During the Civil War, Joseph fought with the regular US Militia, 1st Eng. He married Roxanna A., the daughter of John and Frances Jones, who was born 3 Dec 1840 in ME. By 1870 they were farming 40 acres in sec. 26 of Weston Twp., Clark Co., WI. In 1880 their property adjoined that of George Lloyd to the west, B. F. French to the south, Laura Tracy to the north and **Frank Lavine** to the east. Their son Edwin F. (1865, ME) married Anna Harper 7 Apr 1883 and later moved to a farm in Scollard, OR. They had 6 children; only Bert (1884), Marjorie (1891) and Paul (1899) survived into adulthood. Roxanna passed away 12 Jun 1894 and Joseph died 3 years later, 8 Jul 1897. They are both buried in the Chapel Hill Cemetery of Weston Township.

Francis Marion CARTER 1851 – 1914 ☆ ⚑
VGR #159 dated 22 Feb 1937; Next of kin: Mrs. Frank Carter (Widow)

"Frank" was born 27 April 1851 in Granville, Licking Co., OH, the only child of J. L. Carter. Because his parents died early in his life, Frank moved to Wrightsville, WI to be near relatives. He enlisted with Co. F, 49th Wis. Inf., serving as a "Drummer Boy". His unit left Camp Randall 8 Mar 1865 and reached Benton Barracks, St. Louis, MO, 2 days later. They did guard and garrison duty at Rolla. He was discharged 8 Nov 1865 at St. Louis. Five years later, he lived in Staffordville, WI where he drove a stage line, did lumbering and farmed. Nancy Jane Turnbull became his wife, 22 Feb 1872 in Neillsville, Clark Co., WI. Nancy was born 1 Mar 1854 in Churubusco, Whitley Co., IN. In 1868, at the age of 14, she moved with her parents and 8 siblings to Neillsville. Their son, Claude Jay, was born in Neillsville, 29 Nov 1872.

When Claude was 7 years old, the family moved to Greenwood where he later married Maude, the daughter of Henry W. and Jane (Sheets) Greene, 8 Jan 1906. Claude played with the 32nd Regiment Band under the direction of Theodore Steinmetz and the Greenwood City Band from its organization (1890 ca.) until 1937. He was a trucker for 40 years. Claude's daughter, Iliff (6 Nov 1906) married Mauricio De Pages and moved to Buenos Aires, Argentina.

← **Frank, Nancy and Iliff with "spook"**

Francis M. Carter

Frank and Nancy adopted their 6-yr-old niece, Lida (16 Aug 1888, Bonhome, SD), the daughter of Delbert and Adella "Della" Goodenough. Marian Hodge (Jul 1899, m. Dale Varney), a half-sister of Lida, was apparently adopted by the Carters too. Nancy was a dressmaker with her own millinery shop and behind it she grew flowers (photo above). Frank was an active member of the Modern Woodmen of America and the G.A.R. until his death 24 Aug 1914. The Greenwood Band, of which he had been a member, conducted the cortege to his last resting place. In March 1949 Nancy moved to the Veteran's Home in King where she died the evening of 14 Nov 1951. The Carters, their son and his wife, and Lida, are all buried in the Greenwood, WI City Cemetery.

Caleb Woodworth CHANDLER 1846 - 1925
1885 & 1890 Special WI Veterans Census, Eaton Twp.

"Woody" was born 13 Nov 1846 in Fairfield, Jefferson Co., IA, the son of James M. and Harriet (Woodworth) Chandler. His parents moved to Black River Falls, WI, when he was 2 years old. In 1858, they opened the first grocery store on Water St., operating it for a dozen years, adding dry goods, etc. Woody enlisted as a Pvt. with Co. G, 5th Wis. Inf. 5 Sep 1864 and was honorably discharged 25 May 1865. Five years later, his sister Nettie married his army buddy, **Frank Brown**. The same year, the Chandler and Brown families moved to Clark Co., WI. The following year Woody married Sarah Eliza at the parsonage of Rev. H. W. Bushnell in Neillsville, Sunday, 12 Nov 1871. She was born in Bloomfield, Prince Edward Co., Ontario, Canada, near Pictou, at the head of Quinte Bay. Her parents were John and Hannah (Honeywell) Bowerman. Woody fought hard for an increase in his pension. Interestingly, he'd only spent about 3-4 weeks in actual battle before being hospitalized with dysentery for the rest of the war. He'd been released from the hospital in time to pursue Lee in Petersburgh in April 1865 but a hernia rupture caused a need for further hospitalization. Because of yet another health issue, he'd lost a leg and hobbled around on a crutch most of his life. When he filed for his pension, he stressed only the poverty he was living in. If he'd reported he was a one-legged man, the process would likely have gone much faster. In 1895 the Chandlers and their children: Irvine (15 Nov 1875), Ira (16 Feb 1886), John (20 Feb 1889) and Hazel (23 Jan 1892) were living in Loyal, WI. They later moved to Prince Edward County, Ontario, Canada where Woody died 3 Dec 1925. Sarah passed away 4 Mar 1921. They are both buried in the Cherry Valley Cemetery there.

"**C. W. Chandler**, of this place, who has had his pension papers grinding in the mill for several years, has at last been rewarded with a wind fall in the shape of over 800 shining dollars. It is but just and right that the nation's defenders be rewarded for services rendered." *Neillsville Times, 1882*

John W. CHESTERMAN 1838 - 1928
1895 Special WI Veterans' Census

John was born 29 Jul 1838 in Tuscarawas, OH, the son of Abraham and Susan (Spangler) Chesterman. At the age of 9, he lost his parents. He and his little sister, Mary (1840) then lived with William and Nancy Botkin in Roundhead, OH, where John attended school when he wasn't doing farm work. In the spring of 1853, he went to Fort Wayne, IN. The following summer he began driving on the Wabash & Erie Canal, running to Fort Wayne, Toledo, Lafayette and Cincinnati. The following year he went to Roanoke, cutting cordwood that winter and doing farm labor that summer. He worked in the woods for a lumber company in New Troy, MI, for the next 5-6 years. At the outbreak of the Civil war, he enlisted at Niles, MI., with Co. E, 6th Mich. Inf. and mustered in 20 Aug 1861 under the command of Gen. B. F. Butler. His service included the capture of New Orleans, the battle of Baton Rouge, and doing police work until the siege of Fort Hudson. That battle was nearly continuous from May 23 to July 8, 1863. He then received a 30-day furlough before leaving for Mobile Bay and the taking of Forts Morgan and Gaines. Newly commissioned as Lt., he remained at Fort Morgan shipping ammunition to troops battling at Fort Spanish. He spent the next 6 months with a H.A. Regiment and finally returned to Carlton, LA, to be mustered out. After 4 years of service, he was discharged at Jackson, 20 Aug 1865. With the war behind him, he returned to New Troy, MI. Frances E., a daughter of area farmers, John and Jane (Wood) Morley, became his wife on 7 Dec 1865. She was born at Berrien Springs, MI, 31 Jan 1849. In 1883, the 17th year of their marriage, the Chestermans and their children, Henry M. (26 Aug 1867, lived in Valdez, AK, d. 9 Jul 1937) and Alice (4 Mar 1869, m. John M. Philpott d. 21 Jul 1954) moved to Loyal, WI. In 1889 they purchased their farm in sec. 35, Beaver Twp., Clark Co. WI. Their heavily wooded property, originally granted to C. C. Washburn, had only 3 acres cleared and nothing more than a shack to live in. With his team of horses, John cleared more land. He also built a 7-room home and a nice stock barn. He was a prominent citizen who served on the school board for 6 years. He was secretary of the Beaver Telephone Co. for a year and treasurer for another year. In 1915, John and Frances retired in Loyal, WI. John died 5 Dec 1928 and Frances passed away 14 Aug 1936. All of the family members are buried in the Loyal, WI, City Cemetery.

John Henry CHRISTMAS, Jr. 1845 – 1927 ☆ ⚑

VGR #160 dated 8 March 1937, Next of kin: Mary Bundeson (remarried widow)
1885, Neillsville, Clark Co., WI, 1895 &1890 Special WI Veterans Census, Garden Valley, Jackson Co.

John Christmas

John was born 17 April 1845 in Sandusky, OH, the son of John and Adaline Christmas who were natives of Canada. He moved with them to Lansing, MI, when he was 4 years old. His siblings were Ellen/Helen (1843), Amelia (1847), Henry (1852) and Van (1855). In his 17th year, he enlisted as a Drummer with Co. G of the 12th Mich. Inf., 3 days after Christmas 1863. He stood 5 1/2 ft. tall, had blue eyes, light colored hair and a light complexion. His hand was wounded in a skirmish near Clarinden, 26 June 1864. He was wounded again during the Battle of Gettysburg and twice more after that. He was discharged as a Cpl., 15 Feb 1866 and began drawing a pension 25 Jun 1866. He married Mary Louise Eddy (24 Sep 1850, Eagle, MI, d. 2 Jan 1922, Bradley, SD) in Lansing, MI, about that same year. In 1873 they moved to Neillsville, Clark Co., WI, with their children: Frank E. (2 Feb 1867), Albert Charles (2 Sep 1871), Aiba M. (1875), Claude (2 Apr 1877), Edith L. (1880), Maude Mary (14 Apr 1882), and Eva Amelia (15 Jan 1892, Alma, WI). When the 1880 Census was recorded, John was working as a printer. After a divorce, Mary married Tom Bundeson. John married Clara E. Furing/Furness 2 Mar 1905. We believe Clara E. (1877 ca.), was the daughter of Ole (1844) and Amelia (1853) Furness of Hixton, WI. Her parents had emigrated from Norway and her siblings were Ida O. (1875) and Manferd G. (1880). John and Clara owned a home on Division St. next door to Carl Kleinschmidt and James Fradette. John passed away at his home, 10 Jun 1927, and is buried in the Greenwood City Cemetery.

Francis M. COATS 1829 - 1897
1885 Special WI Veterans' Census, Greenwood

Francis M Coats

Francis was born in Alleghany Co., PA. On 30 Dec 1863, he left farming to join the Union Army as a resident of Dayton, WI, by enlisting in Madison, WI, for 3 years of service. At 35 years he stood 5'11" tall, had blue eyes, light colored hair and a light complexion. He fought as a private in Co. D, 11th Wis. Inf. under Captain Jesse S. Miller. This unit was dubbed "The Richland County Plowboys." Daniel F. Coats of Aiken also fought with this same regiment. Francis was mustered out under telegraphic order, 7 Jul 1865 from the McDougall Hospital, NY, which was near Ft. Schuyler. He'd been admitted there 2 Jun 1865. He and his wife Eleanor were farming in Eaton Twp., Clark Co., WI, when the 1880 Census was taken. At that time their household consisted of their sons Benjamin (1856) and Elijah (1867); daughters Eliza (1867, twin of Elijah) and Anna Greenfield (1854); granddaughters Martha Rigsby (1873), Lydia Davis (1876) and Palley R. Haney (1871). Mary Coats was living in the next household and on 26 Sep 1880 she married Patterson Christie who was also a farmer. Francis was granted his homestead of 120 acres in sec. 30, Eaton Twp. at the Eau Claire land office, 1 Aug 1883. His closest neighbors were Nathan Manes and John Huntzicker. Francis died in Waupaca, WI, 18 Aug 1897.

Jesse C. CRANE 1826 – 1922 ☆ ⚑
VGR#162 dated 27 Feb 1937, Next of kin: Mrs. John Arends of Greenwood

Jesse was born 12 Apr 1826 in Lumberland, Sullivan Co., NY, one of Calvin and Jemima (Quick) Crane's 11 children. He spent his early life on a farm and was a blacksmith. He enlisted with Co. B, 179th Penn. Inf. 16 Oct 1862 serving as a Pvt. and was discharged 27 Jul 1863. He attended the reunion of the Clark Co. Civil War soldiers in Neillsville in June 1903. On 27 Jan 1906 he was elected as a post officer, surgeon, of the Greenwood John A. Eaton Post No. #213. After the close of the war, he moved to WI. In 1870 William H. Begley secured the contract for carrying the mail from Black River Falls, and hired Jesse Crane as his first driver. For many years Jesse worked in the logging camps and literally waded every foot of the Black River from Withee to Black River Falls to prevent the stealing of logs while serving as a guard with the River Police.

When he was 54 years old, Jesse married Mary (Fitch) Pounder of Greenwood, 13 Nov 1880. She was the 52 yr. old widow of Thomas Pounder, with whom she'd had 7 children. Following Mary's death, 4 Apr 1902, Jesse lived with the Shanks family in Greenwood for the last 20 years of his life. He spent most of these years in enfeebled health, unable to work and his gradual decline finally yielded to death, 2 Oct 1922. He had lived to be one of the oldest men in Clark Co., dying at 96 yrs, 5 mo., 16 days. He was buried in the Greenwood, WI City Cemetery.

Charles Henry CUMMINGS 1841 - 1926 ☆ 🏴

VGR #163 dated 3 April 1937, Next of kin: Mrs. John Arends of Greenwood (daughter)

Charles was born 14 Sep 1841 near Springfield, MA, the son of Israel Perkins Cummings (12 Feb 1819) and Mary Priscilla Hale (16 Nov 1816). His father was a native of MA and his mother was born in NY. His siblings were: Wallace E. (Jul 1843, MA – 19 Jul 1905, m. Eunice A.); Israel P. (1845, WI); William L. (Sep 1848, m. Alma), Ida I. (1853, WI) and George (1859, WI). The family moved to WI, in 1844, making the trip across the country by team, and camping along the way, settling in Waushara Co., WI. In 1852, they moved to Weston Twp., Clark Co., WI, to engage in lumbering. They were the 2nd resident family of Weston Twp. Israel killed 128 deer while living there. His wife, with a child in her arms, was lost in the woods during a snow storm, but was saved by neighboring Indians. They then moved to Lincoln, Trempealeau Co. At the age of 21 Charles enlisted at Lincoln, WI, with Co. C, 30th Wis. Inf., 16 Aug 1862, serving as a Pvt. His regiment was assigned to the 2nd Brigade, 2nd Div. Military Dist. of KY. He was sent to Dakota and Minnesota, then south via the Missouri and Mississippi Rivers to Louisville and Bowling Green, KY, where they were put on guard and provost duty. Charles was honorably discharged 5 Oct 1865 at Madison, WI. His brother Wallace fought with Co. D, 36th WI Inf.

After returning home, he and Charlotte F. Fitch where married, 2 Nov 1867. She was born 1 Jan 1846 in Belleville, near Ottawa, Canada. She was fourteen years of age when she came with her mother and younger brother to a place not far from Loyal, WI, where her father and brother had located 2 years before. Not finding it desirable, they moved to Whitehall, WI, in 1860 and to nearby Lincoln before the 1870 census was taken. After Charlotte married Charles, she cooked for lumbering camps where he was foreman. They worked in logging for 32 years. They moved to Greenwood ca. 1871, with their first child. Their children were: Harmettie "Nettie" J. (1868), Louisa M., Eugene (24 Apr 1872), Rue Blanche (9 Sep 1877, d. 10 Oct 1962), Charles William (23 Sep 1883) and Gladys.

They were faithful members of the Methodist Episcopal Church. Charlotte was very interested in the temperance work and joined the W.C.T.U. at the time of its organization ca. 1884. She died 10 Aug 1919 and Charles died at his home 22 Jun 1926. They were both buried in the Greenwood, WI City Cemetery.

Merrill H. DARLING 1848 – 1926 ☆
1885 & 1890 Special WI Veterans' Census, Greenwood

Merrill H. Darling, one of the old residents of Clark County and a veteran of the Civil War who fought with Co. C, 1st Wis. Inf., was born in Madison County, NY, 3 Oct 1848. As a small boy, he moved west with his parents, Dennis and Ann Priscilla (Culver) Darling. The family settled on a farm in WI, where Dennis died when Merrill was just 7 years old. He was the 4th in a family of 6 children. On 2 Nov 1863, at 15 years of age, he enlisted in the Civil War, with Co. C, 1st Wis. Inf. He was honorably discharged at Clinton, IA, 18 Aug 1865. Three of his brothers had also enlisted before him and two of them did not return to civilian life. Darling was married at Fond du Lac, 28 Sep 1882, to Ellen A. Hughes. They moved to Clark County in 1883, and later lived for a time at Thorp. In 1892 they moved to Neillsville. Their children were: Lenn H. (8 Apr 1889, Thorp) and Mabel (May 1887), who both died before their father, and Fred Merrill (5 Jul 1883, Loyal) and Virginia (1904 ca; m. Verne John Smith). Merrill was an industrious upright man, who was intensely patriotic with immense love of his country. For a good many years poor health rendered him unable to work. Merrill was a long-time member of the G.A.R. and remained in good standing until his death, June 27, 1926, after a lingering illness. He and Ellen are both buried in the Neillsville, WI City Cemetery.

Albert Ellsworth DARTON 1844 – 1943 ☆ 🏴
Co. D, 45th WI Inf.; PVT.; 24 Nov 1862-8 Sep1863

Albert, pictured here in his 98th yr., was one of Wisconsin's longest-lived Civil war veterans and the last in the Clark Co. area. From a family of 10 children, Albert was born in Simcoe, Canada, 5 Dec 1844. His family settled at Hartford, WI when he was 4 years old. In his 17th year, his attempt to join the army was blocked when his younger brother, William, Jr., having overheard him and a friend talking about signing up, followed the would-be recruits to Hartford on a cold December day in 1861. While they were talking with Dick Young, of the 17th Wis., William ran back home and told his father who then rode a horse into town and found the boys with the recruiting officer, near the railroad station. The father ordered young Darton to take the horse back home, but Young intervened; "He's my man now, Bill." "If he's your man," Albert's father, **William E. Darton**, replied, "you're a better man than I." In 1861, youths under 18 years needed the parents' consent to enlist. Albert spent the next two years caring for the family farm while his father served. In the spring of 1864, it was Albert's turn to become a soldier and he joined Co. D, 45th Wis. Inf., under Capt. Henry VanEwyk and General Thomas. He always felt his time to serve had been cut because of his brother, William.

As fate would have it, Pvt. Albert Darton was on furlough at the one time he could have seen real action when the 45th defended Nashville, TN from a furious attack led by Gen. Hood. After the war Albert married Ann Eliza Ward, 6 May 1866 in Sheboygan. They farmed in Beaver Twp., Clark Co., living there until retiring in 1919 in the village of Loyal. Ann Darton died 21 May 1928. Albert died at his home in Loyal, 30 Dec 1942. He'd enjoyed splendid health until being confined to bed in his last year. His funeral was in the Methodist church with Rev. M. E. Taylor officiating and Masonic Lodge members attending in a body. Behind the flag-draped casket were members of the American Legion, with Philip Capelle, color bearer of the American Legion flag. Edd Dobbe carried the Legion's emblem banner, with Percy Voight, Leo Meyer, Jesse Raab, and Henry Boe, serving as color guards. Senior Class Pres. Edward Bertz Jr. carried the old flag of the former G.A.R. post. For many years, members of the G.A.R, in a fitting ceremony, had entrusted this same flag into the custody of each succeeding senior class for safekeeping. Albert's death brought that tradition to an end. Despite a severe storm, a large procession accompanied the body to the Greenwood, WI City Cemetery for burial next to Ann who'd died 14 years earlier. Masonic rites were held at the grave and the rituals were delivered by Past Master Clem Rous. The American Legion was represented by County Commander Harry Roehrborn, the County Service Officer, and John M. Peterson of the Neillsville Legion. With a last salute by the Legion firing squad and the sounding of taps by Charles Theisen, Clark County's last Civil War veteran was laid to rest and numbered with our "Grand Army of the Dead."

William E. DARTON 1821 – 1880 ☆ ⌂
VGR#164 dated 27 Feb 1937, Next of kin: Albert Darton of Loyal (son)

William was born 18 Feb 1821, near London, England, the son of Samuel and Ann Darton. He married Sarah Ann (9 Oct 1826, Simcoe, Ontario), the 16 yr. old daughter of John Francis and Elizabeth (Pegg) Braiser. At the time of the 1860 Census, they were farming in Hartford, Washington Co., WI. William joined the Union Army, 24 Nov 1862, enlisting as a Sgt. with Co. I, 34th Wis. Inf. He was discharged 8 Sep 1863. It was a year before he recovered enough to work. The next spring, his oldest son **Albert** (*previous sketch*) enlisted and served until the end of the war. Their children were: Hannah (12 Apr 1843), Albert Ellsworth (5 Dec 1844), Lydia Marie (15 Oct 1846), William E. (24 Nov 1848), Henry J. (25 Sep 1850) Clara M. (4 Jul 1853), Alfred M. (19 Nov 1856), Mary Alwilda (22 Sep 1858), Arthur M. (8 Jun 1866), and Alice (23 May 1868). The first two were born in Canada, and the rest were born in Hartford, WI. William died 11 Dec 1880 and is buried in the Greenwood, WI City Cemetery. Sarah passed away 14 years later, 25 Jul 1894, and was laid to rest at his side.

Jacob W. DAUGHERTY 1837 – 1910 ca. ☆
1890 Special Veteran's Census, Marietta, WI

Jacob (Jun 1837, Adams Co., IL) was the son of Charles (1801, OH, d. 4 Oct 1880, WI) and Elizabeth (1802, NC, d. 15 Feb 1876, WI) Daugherty. His family moved to Grant Co., WI, when he was six years old and two years later resettled in Fennimore. Harriett Jane/Janet (16 Jul 1838, OH) married Jacob, 31 Jan 1858. He was working as a lead miner in Paris, WI. She was the twenty-year old daughter of David Charles and Rhoda (Daniels) Bailey. Two years later the family grew with the birth of the Daugherty's first son, Elmer E. (1862). During Harriett's second pregnancy Jacob enlisted with Co. E, 35th Wis. Inf., 20 Feb 1864. Due to his injuries he was mustered out early, 10 Oct 1864. His two brothers also served: John (2nd Wis. Cav., 1862, died during hospitalization in 1864) and Thomas (25th Wis. Inf., killed at the battle of Resaca, Georgia). Shortly after Jacob returned home, his son John F. (1864) was born. In 1865 the family settled on a homestead near the Wisconsin River in Marietta, Crawford Co., WI. The following year their first daughter, Harriet R. B. "Hattie Belle" (1866) arrived. Huldah J. and Mary L. were born in 1868 after the family had resettled in Ellenboro. They only lived there a year before returning to their Marietta homestead. Death took Mary on a cold winter day, 19 Feb 1871. Christmas had barely passed when their newest baby also died an early death, 29 Dec 1871. Their other children were: George (1872), Adda/Ona/Oney (1875) and Rhoda (1878). "Adda" hadn't reached her 6th year when the family lost her, 28 Nov 1881. In 1902 they moved to Greenwood where their son Edgar was farming. During that time Jacob was an active member of the John A. Eaton G.A.R., serving as Adjt. from 1902-1903. About 1905 they returned to Marietta. The New Year had barely begun when Harriett died 25 Jan 1909. After her death, Jacob lived with his daughter Hulda who'd married John Foust. Both Jacob and Harriett are now buried in Boydtown, WI.

Heinrich DECKER 1835 - 1913 ☆
1885 Special WI Veterans' Census

"Henry" was born 2 Feb 1835, at Hohen-hausen, Lippe Detmold, Germany, the son of Hans Heinrich and Anna Maria (Brandt) Decker. In his 22nd or 23rd year he came to Franklin, Sheboygan Co., WI. He served in the Civil War with Co C., 27th Wis. Inf. from 1862 to 1864. His records indicate he stood 5'9", had blue eyes, light hair and a light complexion. After his return, he married Sophia Wilhelmina Schwarze 13 Oct 1867.

←Henry & Sophia (Schwarze) Decker

She born 19 Feb 1844 and was the daughter of Hans Herman and Sophia (Hover) Schwarze. During May 1870 they heard the call of the northland and left Sheboygan County to establish a homestead in the timberlands of Clark County. They settled on a 240 acre farm in sec. 5 & 6, Warner Twp., about 3 mi. W. of Greenwood where they lived until 1902, when they moved to the Braun Settlement, about 5 mi. north. They were founding members of Warner Evangelical & Reformed Church. With hard labor they built a new home, living there until Henry's death 6 Aug 1913, just a year after Sophia's passing, 1 Aug 1912. Their children were: Anna (18 Jul 1870), Edwin (31 Mar 1872), Gustav (b.13 Mar 1874), Ludwig (21 Aug 1875), Theodore (29 Dec 1876), Auguste Mathilde (4 Nov 1878), Clara Sophie (12 Mar 1881), Alfred Heinrich (3 Jan 1883), and Arthur Friedrich (29 Jan 1886).

Jacob DEMOUTH 1835 - 1905

VGR #527 dated 20 Feb 1937; Next of Kin: Mrs. Clifford Nutting (daughter) of Park Falls, WI

Jacob was born 3 Aug 1835, the son of John and Maria Demouth. He fought as a Pvt. with Co E 21st Wis. Inf. His wife was Cordelia Martindale and they lived in sec. 15 & 16 of Weston Twp. (see Albert Tuttle's bio) When Jacob died 7 Sep 1905, he was buried in Weston's Chapel Hill cemetery. The following are excerpts from a letter written by Dianne Z. Stevens to her Grandchildren concerning Jacob DeMouth of Clark Co., WI.

Dear Sarah and Hannah and Timmy,

I want to tell you a story about your great-great-great grandfathers who fought in the Civil War. His name was Jacob DeMouth and he lived from October 3, 1835 until September 7, 1905.

Jacob was born in Pequat Twp, Morris County, New Jersey, just a few miles from New York City. His parents were John DeMouth and Maria Levi. His DeMouth forefathers had been in this country for many generations. They'd originally come from Alsace Lorraine by way of Holland. Alsace Lorraine is an area that Germany and France fought over for many centuries. Now it is in France and DeMouth is a name that certainly sounds French. His mother was descended from William Levi, a German Jew, who had been brought over as a Hessian soldier to fight in the American Revolution but deserted to the Americans. (The story is he put his shoes on backwards and walked through the snow to the American camp.)

Jacob had five brothers and sisters: Samuel, Chalon, James, Frances, and Semantha. Jacob was between James and Frances. When Jacob was 13 his family moved from New Jersey to Calumet County near Chilton, WI. That was in 1848. In 1861 his father John DeMouth was killed when a tree he had been chopping down fell on him. On August 26, 1861 Jacob married Cordelia Martindale at Gravesville, WI.

Jacob became a soldier on February 26, 1864. He enlisted into Company E, 21st WI Infantry from New Holstein, WI. In May of 1864 Jacob's Company joined General Sherman and fought in the many very bloody battles in Georgia, including Buzzard Roost Gap, Kenesaw Mountain, Marietta, the Siege of Atlanta, the "March to the Sea", and the Siege of Savannah. Savannah surrendered on December 21, 1864, and then Jacob's unit fought several battles in North Carolina. They continued north to Washington D.C. and were in the Grand Review* at the end of the war.

Jacob wrote letters home to his wife, Cordelia...There were some interesting stories told...His granddaughter, Erma, believed he had...the ability to foretell the future and interpret dreams. During the war other soldiers would ask him what their dreams meant. One told of a dream about a grapevine laden with fruit. Jacob said that great good news was in store for him. The next mail brought news that his wife had given birth to a baby boy. Another soldier dreamt of a black cart filled with black apples and drawn by black horses. As the cart bounced along, the apples bounced out but the quantity within the cart was not diminished. Jacob said the dream foretold a very evil event that was to come and would affect not only the dreamer but all people. Within a week they received news that Lincoln had been shot.

After the war Jacob returned to his career as a WI farmer. Sometime around 1870 he moved his family to Christie, Wisconsin near Loyal in Clark County. Jacob and Cordelia had 11 children but only 5 lived to grow up. They were Eva, John, Samuel, Lottie, and Don. Jacob died in 1905 and is buried at Christie with a number of other DeMouths...

Lots of Love From,

Granny

* (see page 120)

Lary DRINKWINE 1821 - 1901 ⭐🏳

VGR #165 dated 27 Feb 1937; Next of Kin: Mrs. Otto Struell (daughter) of Greenwood, WI

Lary was born in Paris, France, 1 May 1821, the son of George Drinkwine, a native of London, England, who brought the family to Montreal, Canada in 1823 where he kept a tavern. After farming until the fall of 1854, Lary moved to Sheboygan Co., WI. He made the voyage on the steamer Lady Elgin, which sprung a leak on the way, obliging the passengers to pump water. They finally landed in the harbor with no loss of life or property. Lary married Clarissa Tedrow, a native of Sherbrook, Canada, in 1851, and worked on a farm near Sheboygan until 1861, when he enlisted with Co. B, 8th Wis. Inf., serving 3 ½ years. He participated in the battles of Mechanicsville, Missouri, Pilot Knob, Luka, Coffeeville, Holly Springs, Corinth, Pine Bluff, the charge on and siege of Vicksburg, the Red River campaign, Guntown, Mississippi, and others. He was wounded 3 times: first on the forehead by a piece of shell on the return from the Red River campaign, next through the left thigh during the charge on Vicksburg, and again in the left ankle at Guntown, the ball striking the bone and passing into the back part of the leg, where it remained lodged the rest of his life. After the war, Lary returned to Sheboygan and worked on a farm until 1865 when he moved his family to Taylor Co., but didn't stay long, moving on to Clark Co., in 1866. Their first home was 12' sq., made of logs and roofed with elm bark, but large enough for their family of five. In 1870 they cleared 80 acres in sec. 20 of Warner Twp. There were no roads to his property and he often walked to and from Neillsville for supplies, camping in the woods on his way. One time he had 50 lbs. of flour on his neck and swam the river because he could not get across by boat. In 1871, the Drinkwines and the families of Thomas Steele, Charles Patterson, Morris Markham, **Curtis Markham** and Baldwin built a log schoolhouse, 16'x 20', chinked the cracks, nicely pointed it up outside with mud and on the inside with lime, and fashioned furniture of lumber. For warmth they stood a big box stove in the center of the room. There were 2 windows on both the north and south sides. The teacher had the west end and the outside door was in the east end. The Drinkwine children were: Lary (Aug 1861), George Washington (4 Mar 1863, m. Maud E. Mabie), John Luther (4 Sep 1864, m. Leone E. Lloyd), Minnie Arvilla "Villa" (1872, m. Otto Gruwell of Greenwood) and Violet (1872). Clarissa died 4 Sep 1896. Five years later, Lary died of pneumonia at 10:30 Wednesday night, 13 Nov 1901 in the home of his daughter. The funeral was held at 10 a.m. in the home. Both he and his wife are buried in the Greenwood, WI City Cemetery.

William M. DUTCHER 1837 - 1922 ☆
1890 Special Wis. Veterans' Census

William was born in 1837 in NY to Ruloff and Sarah Dutcher. In 1850, he was living in Springfield, Otsego Co. NY and in 1860 in Olive, Ulster Co., NY. In 1861 while living in Washington Co., WI, he became one of 220 Union Soldiers who fought with Co. K, 2nd WI Inf. during the Great Civil War. His regiment organized at Camp Randall in Madison, and mustered into service 11 Jun 1861, leaving for Washington, D.C., June 20-26, 1861. From there, they moved into VA, MD, and PA. He fought at Bull Run, defended Washington D.C., Antietam, Chancellorsville, and Gettysburg, and was mustered out 6 Jul 1864. In 1866, shortly after the Civil War, Mary H. Branch became his bride. She too was a native of the "Empire State". They were the parents of 8 children: Willie (m. Albins E. Castner of Loyal, 4 April 1888 and resided in Rapid River, MI), Alice Laure (4 Jun, 1868, M. William Thayer, Jr), Lavina (1870, d. 1881), Lyda; Ruby (1875 d. 1883), Rarda, Sophia (local teacher, m. Fred Gross of Loyal, 16 May 1900), Viola (April, 1883, m. Joe Cline). Both Lavina and Ruby are buried in the Pine Grove Cemetery of Loyal, WI.

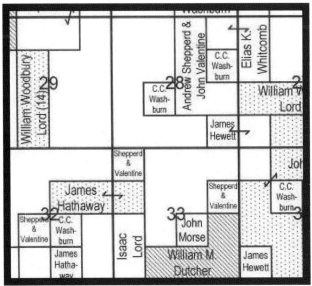

The Dutchers applied for such acreage in section 33 of Beaver Twp., Clark Co., WI, and became the first homesteaders in that township. Their second child, Alice Laure (Thayer) was born 4 Jun 1868, with the distinction of being the first white child born in Beaver Township. The Dutcher family's presence in Beaver Township is recorded on the 1875 WI State Census and the 1880 Federal Census record.

←Dutcher Homestead
Sec. 33, Beaver Township

Any U.S. citizen, or intended citizen, who had never borne arms against the U.S., could file an application, laying claim to 160 acres of surveyed Gov. Land. For the next 5 years, the homesteader had to live on the land and improve it by building a 12' x 14' dwelling and growing crops. After 5 years, the homesteader could file for his patent (or deed of title) by submitting proof of residency and the required improvements. Valid claims were granted ownership to the land free and clear, except for a small registration fee. Title could also be acquired after a 6-month residency and trivial improvements, provided the claimant paid the government $1.25 per acre. After the Civil War, Union soldiers could deduct the time they served from the residency requirements. During the Civil War, William served 3 yrs., 2 mos. and 7 days, and was discharged with a departing rank of 2nd Sgt. The 1905-1910 Federal Census indicates they'd retired from farming and were residents of Greenwood, WI. They were living between the families of Matilda Hogue and Hiley Pratt in 1905 and in 1910 between Alonzo Sheets and Rev. Charles E. Schrein. They were members of the Methodist Episcopal Church. In 1918, the family contributed to the Red Cross effort for World War I. As they aged, William and Mary moved near Granton to live with their daughter Alice and her husband, William Thayer, Jr. and it is there that we found them listed on the 1920 Census. After residing in Clark County for 52 years, William and Mary H. (Branch) Dutcher moved to Portland, OR, to live with their daughter, Viola Cline. William died there 1 Feb 1922. Mary, having spent the remaining 10 years of her life there, died 15 Aug 1929, at the age of 81 years. She did not live to experience any of the great depression which hit 29 Oct 1929. Her demise marked the passing of the last pioneer resident of Beaver Township.

"Wm. Dutcher has sold his flour and feed business to F. J. Klinke, who has moved the stock to his own store." *Greenwood Gleaner 11 May 1900*

Alfred Surraneous EATON 1841 – 1932 ☆

1885 Special WI Veterans' Census

Alfred was the son of Ebenezer and Hannah (Cross) Eaton of Merrimac Co., NH. He was born in Newbury, NH, 13 Aug 1841. He was mustered into the Union Army as a Cpl., 4 Sept 1862, and fought with Co. H, 2nd NH Inf., but was transferred to the 10th NH, and was mustered out as a Capt. in 1865. Greenwood's G.A.R. post #213 was named for **John A. Eaton**, the older brother of Alfred. John never returned home from the war; he died from wounds while serving with Co. H, 10th NH Inf., 27 May 1864. "Major Eaton", as Alfred was called, was a former State Commander of the G.A.R. He became one of Wisconsin's best known Civil War veterans. He married Ann Emmeline Brown in Black River Falls, WI, 12 Oct 1868. She was born 2 May 1849 in Coral City, IL, the daughter of Peris and Achsah (Parks) Brown.

The Eatons had 3 daughters, Viola Adell (1871 – 1966), Fredericka "Freddie" Helen (1879 – 1882) and Genevieve (1882 – 1972). When Alfred left Greenwood in 1892, he relocated in Superior, Douglas Co., WI. Major Eaton died February 10, 1932. He and Emeline are both buried in the Greenwood Cemetery, Superior, Douglas Co., Wisconsin.

Eaton's Hardware Store

The Eaton Family operated a tin and hardware shop in Black River Falls, WI, but it burned in 1871 and $24,000 worth of stock was lost. Shortly afterward they moved to Greenwood, WI to open a new hardware store and by 1881 were offering a large stock of $7,000 and doing a business of $20,000 a year. In 1913 Eaton's Hardware Store was sold to John Schiller.

Jacob John ENHELDER 1831 - 1918
1885 Special WI Veterans Census

Mr. and Mrs. Jacob Enhelder

Jacob was born in Switzerland, 1 Jan 1831, the son of John and Mary Enhelder, who were also the parents of John and Mary. He learned the miller's trade from his father. In 1848, he was the first family member to immigrate to the USA. The 86 day voyage on a sailing vessel terminated at New Orleans. In 1849 he arrived in Clark Co., WI, following an Indian trail from the mouth of the Black River, working in various lumber camps along the way. In 1861, he enlisted with Co G, 10th Wis. Inf. After mustering in at Milwaukee, he was first dispatched to Louisville, KY, and then marched against Beauregard and took part in the battle of Murfreesboro, TN, among others. His brother John fought with the same regiment. After Jacob's return to civilian life in 1864, he married Jessie Douglas, an adopted daughter of Robert Douglas, an old pioneer of Clark Co., WI. He and Jessie lived in Neillsville while he engaged in teaming between Greenwood, Sparta and Neillsville. Later, Jacob was involved with the construction of the railroad before purchasing 80 acres of wild land where a road had been chopped through. He built a log cabin and lived there for three years before trading it for a tract of the same size in sec. 31, Weston Twp., on the west side of the river. There, Jacob built a frame house to accompany the existing barn. They lived there 30 years, raising 6 children: Clarence, Mattie, Dean, Ernest, Willis, and Robert. Jacob took some long walks in the country, occasionally walking from La Crosse to Black River Falls. He died 16 Apr 1918 and is buried in Neillsville, WI City Cemetery. Jessie passed away exactly 13 years later, 16 Apr 1931 and is buried there as well.

Alfred FIELDS 1838 - 1896
1885 Special WI Veterans Census, Greenwood

Alfred's coffin was inscribed with the plain but suggestive word, "Comrade." He fought as a private in Co. A 33rd Wis. Inf. along side his older brother, Bird. He enlisted as a resident of Washburn, Grant Co., WI, 21 Aug 1862 with the Union forces for 3 years and was paid a $25 bounty. Pvt. Fields was 22 years old, had blue eyes, light hair and a fair complexion, stood 5'10" tall and had a slender build. He was honorably discharged 14 Apr 1863.

Alfred Fields

Alfred was born in Randolph Co., IN in 1838, the son of Dempsey (1810) and Lydia (Tucker) Fields. Alfred married Emily Taylor (ca 1840) about 1863 and they had 3 children: Wesly Lester, Clara and Laura. Emily's sister married Bird Fields, Alfred's brother. His second wife was Emma Coats (Jun 1860) and they had 5 children: Fred, Elmer, Charles, Elsie and a premature infant who died because of some heavy lifting by Emily. Alfred died 28 Mar 1896 when he was 57 years old and was buried in the Levis Twp. Cemetery, Clark Co., WI. Emma died in 29 Mar 1935 in Centralia, Lewis Co., WA.

John Tyler FOUST 1841 – 1917 ☆

Attended the 1903 Reunion for Clark & Wood Counties, w/Greenwood Address

John was born 5 Mar 1841, in Randolph Co., IN, the son of John Almarion Tyler and Elizabeth (Loy) Foust. His parents were born in Campbell Co. (now Union), TN. The family had moved to WI, in the early 1860s and made Crawford Co. their home. John spent his 24th birthday in the state of his mother's birth doing guard duty with Co. H of the 44th Wis. Inf. He served under Capt. Levi Houts, a 38 yr. old school teacher from Orion, WI. Four days later his regiment left Nashville to escort prisoners from Eastport, MS, but returned to Tennessee without them because they hadn't been delivered to the relay location. April 3rd he left for picket duty in Paducah, KY, and remained there until 9 Aug 1865 when he was mustered out. His brother Martin and brother-in-law **Zephaniah Silvers** (m. Louisa Catherine Foust) served in the same unit. Just before his 25th birthday he married Margrietta "Louisa" (Aug 1846, WI) in Boydtown, WI, 15 Feb 1866. Her parents, William and Mary Wayne, were from the Bluegrass State which had become familiar ground to John during the Civil War. The Waynes lived in Prairie Du Chien, WI. To their joy all 10 of Louisa and John's children were also born in Crawford Co., WI. Cyrena E. "Rena" (Feb 1867) married the son of **Jacob Daugherty**, Edward D., 4 Feb 1885 in Marietta, WI. Their twins, Altha M. & Weltha L. died the same day (Apr 1869, d. 24 Sep 1879). David E. (24 Mar 1871-1939) married Mary E. McKinsley, 13 Sep 1893 in Marietta, WI. George Martin (5 Aug 1874-24 Feb 1917) married Leila Alvina Lloyd, 26 Oct 1899 in Loyal, WI. Estella I. (15 Feb 1876-15 Jan 1967) married Dwelly P. Bush, 30 Nov 1895 in Marietta, WI. John Allen (Jan 1880-27 Mar 1942) married Polly Foster in 1903. Wallace B. was born 2 Oct 1882 and died 26 Sep 1915 in Marietta, WI. Mary I. was born 19 Sep 1885 and died 16 Mar 1888 in Marietta, WI, and Chester Z. was born 21 Jul 1889 and died Mar 1964. John's father moved to Warner Twp. from Black River Falls in 1908 and rented the old "Yankee Farm." John T. and Louisa were already living in Longwood, WI, and he was active in the John A. Eaton G.A.R. Post in Greenwood, serving as an officer as early as 1906. John Jr. died 17 Apr 1917 and Louisa passed away two weeks later. Both of them are buried in the Boydtown Cemetery.

Daniel S. FRANCIS 1844 - 1926 ☆ 🏳

VGR#168, 27 Feb 1937; Next of kin: Fanny Wollenberg, 10525 Hale Ave., Chicago, IL (daughter)

Daniel was born 17 Nov 1844, the son of George W. and Fanny Francis. His father was a native of MA and was a carpenter and his mother was a dressmaker. The family was raised in Sutton, Merrimac, NH. Daniel's older brother was George A. (1841) and his younger brother was Samuel J. (1847). He also had two sisters, Franny Janet (1853) and Carrie L. (1855). Daniel enlisted with Co. H of the 2nd Regiment of the NH Inf., 27 May 1861. This was the same unit that **Alfred Eaton** served with. Pvt. Francis' first action was at Bull Run, VA, followed by the Siege of Yorktown, Williamsburg, a Skirmish at Fair Oaks. He also fought in the 2nd Battle of Bull Run, Fredericksburg and Gettysburg where he was severely wounded. After being honorably discharged 21 June 1864, he immediately applied for his pension because of the injuries he'd sustained. His brother George had also joined the Union Army in the fall of 1861 and fought with Co. H, 4th NH Inf. Daniel was both a woodsman and laborer. Margaret J. became Daniel's wife in Pierce Co., WI, 2 Feb 1868. She was born in NY, Oct 1854 to an Irish father and a Scottish mother. We believe her parents were Peter and Margaret Green. Margaret and Daniel farmed in Spring Lake and had an estate valued at $400 in 1870. The nearest Post Office was in Rock Elm. Their children were all born in Spring Lake, WI: William (1868-1870), William C. (Nov 1870, m. Ora Adams) and their twins born in June 1875–Fanny B. "Frankie" (m. Edward F., the son of **Chris Wollenberg**) and Herbert A. By 1880 they were farming in Thorp, WI, on a homestead in Sec. 34 which was later issued to "David L. Francis" 15 Jan 1884 at the Eau Claire Land Office. They later moved to Greenwood where both Herbert and Fanny taught in the local schools. Margaret died 28 May 1925 after a long illness. At the time of his death, Daniel was nearly 82 years old. He'd been up and around as usual until about 6 pm Thursday evening 22 Apr 1926 when he became ill. Medical aid was summoned but he passed away at home early the next morning. Their funeral were both held in the home they were buried beside one another in the Greenwood, WI City Cemetery.

William C. FRICKE 1820 – 1897 🏴

William was born 17 Feb 1820, in Diepholz, Germany, the son of Christopher and Christina (Nolte) Fricke, both natives of Germany. William was a soldier in the German Revolution (1848-49), having fought against the king in favor of a republic. When that effort failed, he with others took passage on a ship to the USA, stopping first in Milwaukee in the fall of 1849. He worked at the shoemaker's trade until the summer of 1850, and then moved to Newburg, WI, to work at his trade until 1855. His marriage to Eva took place 9 Aug 1852. She was born 15 Mar 1830, the daughter of Gotfried and Justine (Dobig) Fretsche. Three years later they moved to Waco, TX, but returned to Newburg two years later. During the Civil War, he served as a Corp. with Co. B, 3rd Wis. Inf. having enlisted 20 Aug 1864 for 3 years of service as a substitute. At that time, he was 24 years old, 5', 7" tall, had a dark complexion, brown eyes and brown hair. Because of the close of the war, he was mustered out 18 Jul 1865 at Madison, WI. In 1876, he settled his family on 80 acres in sec. 26, Eaton Twp., Clark Co., WI. The Frickes had 12 children, but only 10 lived to adulthood: Ida, Minnie, Oscar, Emma, William, Matilda, Louise, Bertha, Robert who died at the age of 24 in Milwaukee, and Otto who died 15 Apr 1880 when he was 20 years old. Politically, William was a Democrat and twice he was a member of the Town Board and also served on the School Board for several years. The village of Greenwood was incorporated as a city 2 Apr 1891 and when the first election was held, William and another Civil War Veteran, **Robert McCalvy**, were the Ballot Clerks. Eva died 9 Jul 1901 and William died 17 Feb 1897. Both of them are buried in the Greenwood City Cemetery.

Cortes/Cortez J. GATES 1848 - 1895 ☆
1885 & 1890 Special WI Veterans' Census, Christie

Cortes was born in NY, the son of Aaron C. and Maria Gates, farmers who moved from the "Empire State" to claim a homestead in Vernon Co., WI, at the land office in La Crosse, 10 Sep 1860. That year, Cortes was recorded as a 17 yr. old resident of Minerva, Essex, NY. His father, Aaron was a veteran of the War of 1812 who lived to the ripe old age of 89 years and he is buried in the Neillsville, WI City Cemetery. He and Maria had three sons, Cortes J., Sylvanus (1852) and George (1856). During the Civil War, Cortes fought with three successive units: 16th NY H.A. (mustered in Sep 1863 at Troy, Buffalo, NY, and transferred

May 1864); Co. H, 1st NY Mounted Rifles; and Co. A, 4th NY Provisional Calvary (a consolidation of the 3rd Cavalry and the 1st Mounted Rifles, 6 Sep 1865, with an honorable discharge 29 Nov 1865). Shortly after the war 5 Dec 1866, Cortez applied for an invalid's pension. At the time of the 1870 Census, Cortes was recorded as 29 years old, farming with his aunt and uncle, Daniel and Jane (Hewett) Gates in Clark Co., WI. "Dan" and Jane had located at the mouth of Wedges' Creek where he kept a well known and popular log tavern, resort and resting place in Levis Twp. until about 1861. The horse team with which Mr. Gates hauled his freight from Sparta, WI, were among the first horses seen in the county, he and his family traveling by stage. In 1861 he purchased 20 acres of land on a site adjoining the suburbs of Neillsville where he erected a log house, sided over, and a large frame barn. The land was all wild and uncultivated. Cortes not only cleared it, but even purchased additional land. Cortes married Jane A. Kimball 21 Jun 1874, in Clark Co., WI. She was born during 1844. They were the parents of a daughter, Elsie Frances (13 Apr 1875; m. Lorenzo Fayette Wood). By 1880, the family had settled on a farm in sec. 32 of present day Eaton Twp. Cortes' parents and his brother George lived with them. Extended family members also settled in sec. 11, Eaton and some in sec. 15 of Weston Twp. During the winter of 1884, Cortes was "putting in logs" for James Reddan in Eaton Twp. and made the local news when he reported hauling a log to the Black River, measuring 18 feet long and four feet across inside the sap at the top end. It scaled at 1860 board feet. Cortes died before 28 Jan 1895, and is buried in the G.A.R. section of the Neillsville, WI City Cemetery. Jane died at the age of 53 yrs., 19 Mar 1897 in Merrillan, WI.

Ebulius Grover HARTSON 1815 – 1892 ☆ ⚑
VGR#170 dated 27 Feb 1937, Next of Kin, H. H. Hartson (son)

Ebulius was born in Otsego Co., NY, 4 May 1815, the son of David and Olive (Rice) Hartson. His parents are thought to have been the first settlers of Paris, NY. The family left for Trumbull Co., Ohio, soon after 1820. Ebulius enlisted with Co. E, 41st Wis. Inf., 8 May 1864 and was mustered in 8 Jun 1864, moving to Memphis TN, by the 15th to be attached to the 2nd Brigade. They did garrison, railroad guard and picket duty until September. August 21 they repulsed Forest's attack. Ebulis served as a Pvt. And received a honorable discharge, 23 Sep 1864. The daughter of Joseph and Nancy Chamberlain, Mary Ann (Rublee) married Ebulius, in Sugar Creek, Walworth Co., WI, 9 Sep 1850. She was born in Newbury, Orange Co., VT, 13 Apr 1815. The Hartsons were the parents of Albert A. (1852, Elkhorn, WI), Eveline (7 Dec 1854), Henry Hobart (24 Jul 1856, Newchester, Adams Co., WI) and Maggie (12 May 1869, adopted). The family is listed on the 1860 Census for Trenton, Washington Co., WI, and on the 1870 Census for Marion, Juneau Co., WI, and by the time of the 1880 Census, they were living in Grant Twp., Clark Co., WI. Ebulius died 4 Dec 1892 and Mary Ann passed away 1 Dec 1901. They were buried in the Greenwood, WI City Cemetery.

John R. HOFFMAN 1844 - 1923 ☆ ⚑
VGR#171 dated 27 Feb 1937; Next of Kin: Mrs. Wm. Nevil (daughter) of Neillsville, WI

John was born 13 June 1844 in Kloton, Zurich, Switzerland, the son of Jacob (1811 - 1888) and Barbara (Hintermeister) Hoffman. In 1851 he immigrated to America with his parents, settling on a farm in Stockbridge, Calumet Co., WI. His siblings were Paulina (1851),

Amanda (1854) and Henry W. (1868). John worked with his father until he purchased the McMahon farm on the 26 Road, 4 miles South of Greenwood in sec. 22, near the Eaton Ctr. School, taking possession 1 Apr 1900. Later he moved into Greenwood, where he resided until his death 30 Jun 1923, at the ripe old age of 79 years and 17 days. During the Civil War he served as private in Co. E., 21st Wis. Inf. He married Anna M. Bertz of Fond du Lac 21 April 1873. They had two daughters: Emma (1874) and Ida A. (Dec 1875, m. Michael Neville, 6 Jan 1904). Anna died 1 Sep 1912. In 1914 John married a widow, May E. Clermont (Oct 1869, IL) of Jefferson, Cole Co., MO. He passed away 30 Jun 1923 and was laid to rest in the Greenwood, WI City Cemetery where Anna and their adopted son, Glen W. (16 Apr 1887, d. 30 Dec 1910) are also buried.

"John Hoffman who some time ago purchased the McMahon farm is expected to arrive this week."
Greenwood Gleaner, 6 Apr 1900

Charles Patterson HOGUE 1844 - 1931 ☆ ⚐
VGR#172 dated 27 Feb 1937, Next of kin: W. E. Hogue (son)

Charles was born 26 Feb 1844 in Hopewell Twp., PA, the son of James Patterson and Sarah (Sunderland) Hogue. His parents were also natives of the Keystone State. His family moved to Sparta, Monroe Co., WI, in 1853. While living in Sparta, WI, Charles enlisted as a Pvt. with Co H, 10th Inf. Wis., and was later promoted to Full Cpl. He transferred into Co E, 21st Wis. Inf., 10 Oct 1861 and then into the 3rd Wis. Inf., 8 Jun 1865. He was honorably discharged July 18, 1865. Three years later, he married Nellie Matilda Potter, 20 Apr 1868. She was born 4 Apr 1847 in Union Twp., Rock Co., WI.

The Indians were friendly and did not disturb the early settlers, though many were afraid of them as the following story will prove. In 1873 Charles Hogue lived about six miles northeast of Greenwood on what was later known as the Lloyd farm. One day when Mrs. Hogue and her two small children were home alone she heard a noise at the door. When she opened it, there stood an Indian with bloody hands. She was so frightened that she grabbed the baby (Oscar) and pretended she was going to get some wood, picked up Harry, who was in the yard, and ran with the two children through the clearing into the woods to the nearest neighbor about two miles away. The Indian called to her as she ran which only frightened her more. She remained there until evening when the neighbor (who was a grandfather of Sena Hanson) fired his gun several times, and Mr. Hogue, returning home about this time knew it was a signal, and went there, found his family and brought them home. Later this Indian told Mr. Hogue that he had killed a deer in the edge of the clearing and wanted to trade part of the meat for groceries, and that he realized Mrs. Hogue was frightened and called to reassure her. While "shooting the rapids" at the "Rips" in a boat, Charles Hogue (who was at time considered the best boatman on the river) was upset into it. He was under so long the men said: "Well, I guess Charley is gone this time", but he finally came up quite a ways down the river under the boat but managed to get out and reach shore safely. *"Greenwood, Hub of Clark Co. WI"*

William Welsch, with the assistance of Frank Brown, Charles Hogue, and Oscar Nutting surveyed and platted the village of Greenwood, 6 Jun1871. The Hogues were some of Greenwood's earliest pioneers and their son, Harry was a charter member of the St. Mary's Parish. The Hogues were the parents of: Harry (1869), Oscar (1872), William (1874), Pearl (1876, m. Simerson), Ray Everett (1878), Stella (m. O'Conner), Nellie M.

(m. Buhite), Ethel (m. Tripp), and Dellame. Charles died 24 Feb 1931 and is buried in the Greenwood, WI City Cemetery. Nellie Matilda passed away at her home, 771 E. Belmont St., Portland, OR, 11 Jul 1930.

Phillip P. HOWARD 1836 - 1918 ☆

1895 Special WI Veterans Census, Greenwood

Phillip was born 1836 in France to George and Magdalena Howard. He fought with Co H, 32nd Wis., Inf. This Regiment was organized at Camp Randall, Madison, WI. He enlisted 14 Aug 1862 and mustered into service Dec 1862. Pvt. Howard had blue eyes, brown hair, light complexion, and was 5' 10 1/2" tall. The soldiers moved to Columbus, KY, from 31 Jan to 2 Feb, 1863. Co. "H" detached to Memphis, TN 12 May, then reunited with the regiment at Cairo, IL, 14 Aug and returned to WI 16 Aug 1865 to be mustered out of service. His regiment lost 1 officer and 18 enlisted men by disease. Catherine Southard (1840, d. Aug 1891) was Phillip's first wife. They married 22 Mar 1868 and their children were: Clara Francis (22 Apr 1871), Ella E (28 Jul 1869, d. 8 Jan 1891) and Lily May (d. 19 Dec 1867). At the turn of the century, Phillip moved from his home in Medford, WI, to the "Old Soldiers' Home" in Waupaca, 11 Feb 1899. Rhoda "Maria" Olin, the former wife of George H. Keeler (1845, MI), AKA Geo. H. Clay, lived with Phillip as his wife. Her first husband had deserted and then re-enlisted with the Union Army in Michigan.

Phillip P. Howard

She never legally divorced George because his whereabouts were unknown. Consequently, her 2nd marriage to Smith Hunter was not valid and he'd died in MI. Therefore, she and Phillip were not legally married either because she was technically still married to her first husband, George. Maria was born 13 May 1840 in Newark, NY*, and had been admitted to the home 29 Dec 1897, as the wife of Clifford Olin. Her first husband, George, died at the Waupaca Veterans' Home and is buried there. Phillip and Maria left the home in May 1910. Phillip died in Waupaca, WI, on 15 Jun 1918 and was buried at Lakeside Cemetery, Waupaca, WI.

*1870 Crystal Lake, MI Census Records indicate Maria was born 1848 in MI.

George Washington HUBBELL 1829 - 1902
1885 Special WI Veterans' Census, Greenwood

George was born 25 Jul 1829 at Hancock, NY, and moved to Honesdale, PA, with his parents. In Waymart, PA, he married Jenny H. Stanton (Jan 1831, PA) in 1850 at Waymart, PA. In 1863 he fought as a Capt. for the bold "Wayne Co. Conscripts". He rose to the rank of Major and Paymaster, before receiving his honorable discharge. He ran the gauntlet of Hood's besieging rebels with 3 strongboxes of money on a flying locomotive and drifting raft, with one guard, and his only shelter the cottonwood boughs piled over his raft – a volunteered service for his colonel, Crane. When offered the charge of a regiment, he exclaimed, "What! Get killed and have my name spelled wrong in the papers, so that the folks at home won't know whether I'm dead or alive?" But he took the command and made a hot streak for the enemy. Soon after the war he went to TN to manage a plantation and the locals destroyed his property. They forced him onto a scaffold and put a noose around his neck, but his coolness amused them and they turned him loose. In 1869, he arrived in Greenwood, WI. His family followed in 1871, with an interval of 8 years spent in MT, and some years in Fifield, WI. He was lured to Clark Co., WI, by his half-brother, J. L. Keator of Rock Island, IL, to manage his Black River extensive logging operations. Prior to his death he suffered greatly, with the exception of his closing days when he remarked to his wife that he did not know it was so exceedingly easy to die. He died of consumption 3 Aug 1902 and was buried in the Neillsville, WI City Cemetery. The Hubble children were: Clara B. (Jul 1855, PA, m. Freeman D. Lindsay); William S. (1861, IL), and Fred K. (1873, WI).

Rudolph Samuel HUMMEL 1837-1919 ☆

Rudolph resided in sec. 22, Warner Twp, Clark Co, WI. He was born in Dorf, Brugg County, Switzerland, on Christmas Day, 1837. His mother died when he was small. In 1850, his father brought the family to Cleveland, OH, but died 2 yrs. later. Rudolph remained a year with his stepmother before locating in Waukesha, WI, in 1855. The next spring he moved to Clark Co., where he remained at Levi's Tavern until that fall. He then went to Alma Center and on to Hixton, Jackson Co., in 1859. In 1860 he was living in Black River Falls, where he enlisted in the Union army, Sep 1861, in Co. G, 16th Wis. Vol. Inf. He served until Feb 1863, but was discharged for disability, having received a gunshot wound in his left arm. He participated in the battles of Perryville, Bowling Green, Murfreesborough, Bridgeport, Bear Creek, Stevenson and others. In the fall of 1864 Rudolph re-enlisted in Co. G, 5th WI, Inf. and served until the close of the war. He was in the battles of Hatcher's Run, Petersburg, Sailor's Creek and others. His wound never healed and he later drew a pension. After the war Rudolph returned to Black River Falls to drive a team for D. J. Spaulding and in 1872, he homesteaded 80 acres in sec. 30, Beaver Twp.

Rudolph settled on a heavily timbered farm in 1882. He married Louisa Hepsia Schermerhorn, who was born in Erie Co., NY, 20 Apr 1863. They had 5 children: William G. (m. Almeda Baker), Warren I. and Oscar A., Albertus J. who died 19 Feb 1890 at the age 23 yrs, and their daughter, Myrtle who died 21 Oct 1886, at 7 yrs of age. The Hummels also adopted Laura L. Rudolph. Politically he was a Republican and he belonged to the G.A.R. The family worshipped at the Methodist Episcopal Church. Louisa died January 1, 1912, and was laid to rest in the Multnomah Park Pioneer Cemetery, Grave#1, Lot 36. Rudolph died 29 Jun 1919 and was buried next to her.

James JEFFERSON 1844 - 1917 ☆
1890 Special WI State Census for Veterans, Eaton Twp., Clark Co., WI

James was born 6 Feb 1844, in Canada, the son of John & Hannah (McCamb) Jefferson who farmed in Monroe, Adams Co., WI. The family immigrated to the USA from Downie, Perth Co., Ontario in 1856. Their children were: William, John, James, Eleanor, George, Mary Ann, and Elias. When he enlisted in the Civil War 17 Aug 1864, he was living in Sugar Creek, WI. He fought as a Pvt. with Co K, 38th WI, Inf. through 2 Jun 1865 and as a result suffered a permanent hearing loss. James married Lorian Adella Hinkley, the daughter of Charles Gale & Pamelia A. (Comstock) Hinkley, on 4 Jul 1868. Their children were: Gertrude Imogene (Nov 1869; m. DeWitt Elwood), Lorian Pamelia (Oct 1872), James Edgar (Jul 1877; m. (1) Susie Eliza Wilbur, d. 1912; m. (2) Bertha M. Moore), and Harry Asbury (Oct 1880; m. Jeanette Joyce). He was a minister at the Greenwood, WI, Methodist Church (1889-1891). While living in Greenwood, he was likely a member of the John A. Eaton G.A.R. Post #213, since it was established in 1885. He served as minister in many Wisconsin towns, including Gratiot, Patch Grove, De Soto, Dunn, and Richwood. His son Harry became a physician and both of his daughters graduated from Lawrence College, Appleton, WI. James died 26 Jul 1917 and was buried at Walnut Hill Cemetery, Baraboo, WI, sec. K, with a G.A.R. signification. Lorian Adella was living in Flint, MI, with the family of her son Harry when she passed away 13 Aug 1930. She was buried beside her husband.

Martin Luther JENKINS 1839-1928 ☆ 🏳
VGR#173 dated 27 Feb 1937; Next of Kin: Geo. Jenkins (son) of Greenwood, WI

Martin L Jenkins

Martin was born in Ellisburgh, NY, 22 May 1839, the son of Luther and Lydia Brit (Wood) Jenkins. He enlisted in the Civil War at Menasha, WI, in 1861, with Co C. 10th WI, Inf. and was mustered in at Milwaukee Nov 1864. Pvt. Jenkins was 5'9 ¾" tall, had blue eyes, brown hair and a light complexion. He was wounded two times.

Martin Jenkins

Martin's first injury occurred at the battle of Stone River when he took a bullet in his left jaw and secondly, he was shot in his left ankle at Chickamauga. On 16 Nov 1863, Helen Amelia Scott became Martin's wife. She was born in Jefferson Co, NY, 5 Nov 1842, the daughter of Ephraim W. and Sarah (Averil) Scott. The Jenkins Family lived in Chilton and Brothertown, WI, before moving to Clark Co., WI, around 1900. They lived in Sec. 35, Eaton Twp. and owned 226 acres. Helen and Martin were the parents of 3 children: Ralph M. (15 Jan. 1866), George H. (29 Sept 1872) and Mary A. (21 Aug 1874).Martin was forced to give up farming because he was crippled in both legs by rheumatism and bed-ridden following a fall in Oct. 1922. Helen died 29 Mar 1922 and Martin passed away at his home in Greenwood, 24 Feb 1928. His Funeral was held at the Methodist Church and his body was laid to rest in the Greenwood, WI City Cemetery.

Charles KAYHART 1844 - 1909
1885 & 1890 Special WI Veterans' Census, Weston Twp.

Charles was born at Boonton, N.J., March 23, 1844, and at the age of 18, enlisted with Co. F, 27th N.J. Inf., serving his country until July 2, 1863. He later drew a pension as an invalid, 13 Nov 1890. After his discharge he returned to New Jersey, residing there until about 1869, when he moved to Calumet Co. WI. His brother Hiram fought with Co. K, 7th NJ Inf. Charles came to Clark County 11 Apr 1871, settling on a farm in sec. 23, Weston Twp. Another Civil War Soldier, **Charles Roseman** was his closest neighbor. He married Harriet E. 31 May 1853, the daughter of Edward (5 Oct 1830) and Amanda (Barnes) Smith. The Kayhart children were: Una (m. Christopher Musselman); Amanda "Amy" (12 Feb 1873, m. Fred Draper), Neva (3 Dec 1876, m. Wm. Swann) and Roy L. (7 Nov 1878, m. Nellie B. Ward). About 8 am, 2 Aug 1909, Charles and son Roy were going to unload some hay. Charles told his son he'd set the hay light, as it had settled making too heavy a load. He set the fork in the back part of the wagon and stepped to the front end as the team started. The forkful of hay, instead of dividing near the center, as expected, strung clear across the load, causing Charles to lose his balance, throwing him to the floor, a distance of nine feet, where he struck on his left temple. He was picked up unconscious, carried to the house and despite medical aid; he passed away the next evening. He was buried in the Neillsville, WI City Cemetery. Hattie passed away 1 Sep 1936 and was laid to rest at his side.

Humphrey Cornelius KETCHUM 1844 - 1909
1885 Special WI Census for Veterans, Christie, Weston Twp., Clark Co

"Humphrey" was born near Duanesburg, Schenatady Co., NY, 9 Oct 1844 to Jesse and Eliza Ketchum, who were also natives of the "Empire State." His brothers were Augustus (1840), William (1842), Henry (1843) and his sister was Abigail (1849). Humphrey enlisted at Chicago 11 Mar 1865 as a Pvt. with Co. K, 9th IL Cav. He received an honorable discharge 27 Oct 1865 and was mustered out at Selma, AL, four days later, 31 Oct 1865. He married Phebe T. 29 Oct 1872 in Clark Co., WI. She was born in Wisconsin about 1849. Their children were: Clarence Maines (1869, Step-son), Forest H. (1874, m. Cora Ellen McGill, d. 24 Aug 1952 in Boulder, CO), and Lewis (1878). He filed for an invalid pension, 6 Jul 1885. Humphrey died 6 May 1909 and is buried in Rose Hill Cemetery, Rifle, Garfield Co., CO. Phebe filed for a widow's pension 8 May 1909 in CO.

Peter F. LANTZ 1833 - 1910 ☆
1885 & 1890 Special WI Veterans Census & VGR #556, dated 5 Mar 1937

Peter was born in Metz, Ger., near the Rhine, 13 Feb 1833. His father, George P. Lantz, a stone mason, brought his family to the United States in 1838, settling in Detroit, MI, where Peter was raised and educated. Mary J. Sheldon, sister of **Frederick J. Sheldon**, married him 2 Jan 1855 in MI. She was born in Onondaga Co., NY, 1 Apr 1833. On 7 Aug 1862, at age 26, Peter enlisted as a Pvt. with Co. D, 24th Mich. Inf. serving 10 mos. in the Civil War. He was in the battles of Fredericksburg, Port Royal and Front Royal, and never received a wound, but received a disability discharge 4 June 1863 at White Oak Church, VA, due to asthma. He returned to farming in Detroit before moving to Clark Co., WI, Mar 1882. He purchased 80 acres, 25 of it cleared, near Longwood Twp., sec. 27 & 28, and was a neighbor to **John McCarty** and **Fred Sheldon**. Peter & Mary had 5 sons: John A. (died age 1), Perry A. (1852), George F. (1858), Walter A. (1868) and Bradley E. (1871). Perry married Ellen Bogue, and lived in Newaygo Co., MI. George lived in Vancouver, WA, and married Ellen McCarty. Walter, a printer in Chicago, married Florence L. Taylor. Bradley married Maude Carlin. In 1883 Peter began receiving a pension because he suffered with rheumatism and bronchitis. He was a Republican and a member of the G.A.R. Mary Jane was a member of the Woman's Relief Corps. Peter died in Thorp, WI, 16 Jun 1910, after a long illness, and was buried in the Thorp Village Cemetery. Mary Jane passed away at the home of her son Bradley at Rice Lake, WI, 27 Dec 1915. Her remains were brought to the home of S. S. Warner of Thorp. After a funeral at the M. E. Church, she was buried beside Peter. A new Civil War marker was placed on Peter's grave by the Thorp American Legion and the Clark Co., WI History Buffs and dedicated 4 Jul 2006 by the community.*

"P. F. Lantz and wife were down from Longwood Tuesday visiting with **Christian Wollenberg** and family." *Greenwood Gleaner, 6 Apr 1900*

*see pg. 117

Franklin LAVINE 1846 - 1932
1885 & 1895 Special WI Veterans' Census

Taps sounded for "Frank" 4 May 1932. Amid a circle of bowed, uncovered heads, the final salute was fired. He'd died the 30th of April and was one of the last "Boys in Blue" to be laid to rest in Clark Co., WI. He was born in NY during Mar 1846. Shortly after his arrival in WI he joined Co E, 19th Wis. Inf. in 1862. He served 2 years and fought at Bull Run and Gettysburg. Illness brought him an early discharge. He always treasured his memories of seeing Lincoln and Grant. After his service, he homesteaded in sec. 26 of Weston Twp. with his French Canadian parents, Franklin Sr. (1803) and Olive (1816) Lavine. His siblings were Mathilda (1850, NY); Joseph (1855, WI); Alfred (1856, WI); William (1863, WI), and Maggie (1863, NY, adopted). Their closest neighbor was **Plyna Shepard**. Late in life, Frank married the widow of George Hotelling, Georgiana; she died 23 Apr 1908. His retirement years were spent in Neillsville where he was a member of the Odd Fellows and lived with his cousin, William Lapp. Both Georgiana and "Frank" are buried in the Neillsville, WI City Cemetery.

William Henry MARDEN 1845 – 1912
1885 Special WI Veterans' Census

William H Mardin

William, "the hunter", was born 12 Mar, 1845, in Upper Canada, 50 miles from Quebec, the son of Joseph A. and Lucy (Annis) Marden. Both parents were natives of MA, who settled in Richland Co., WI in 1854. They raised 11 children: Clifton S., Riley, Joseph A., Mary E., Alfred C., William Henry, Lorenzo D., Edwin J., Hattie, Alberto L., and Solomon S. Growing up on the family farm, William learned the blacksmith's trade, following it 12 years. During the Civil war he served a year in Co. K, 2nd Wis. Inf. and was taken prisoner at the battle of Bull Run, and held 10 months. He was paroled, exchanged and discharged.

He then re-enlisted 1 Oct 1863, in Co. A, 30th Wis. Inf. and served until 20 Sept., 1865 before being honorably discharged in Louisville, KY. Pvt. Marden had blue eyes, brown hair, a fair complexion and stood 5'11" tall. He was in many battles including Nashville, Shiloh, Baton Rouge, and he even confronted the Indians. Seven of his brothers also served. In the fall of 1865 he moved to Richland Co., WI, but traveled most of a year. Charlotte, the daughter of George D. and Dorcas (Riser) Williams of Richland, became his bride 18 Nov 1866. She was born in Marion Co., OH 8 Sep, 1846. Her siblings were: Olive, Edward, Nancy, Polly, W. Jackson, Caroline, and who John died as a prisoner at Andersonville during the war. William and Charlotte raised 10 children: George Henry (16 Dec 1867), Mary Jane (30 Nov 1869), William Wallace (22 Mar 1875), Leslie Seymour (15 Aug 1876), Charles Henry (8 Dec 1877), Ira Taylor (30 Jun 1880), Steven A. (19 Sep 1881), James Edward (5 Dec 1882), Cora E. (28 Dec 1883), and Benjamin (1 Feb 1884). William resided in Richland Co., WI, until 1877, except for 3 years spent in OH. In 1877, he entered a homestead claim for 45 acres of densely forested land in sec. 2, Weston Twp. William's family says he tended to reorganize the truth and to shave some years off his age in an attempt to seem younger than he actually was. You can be the judge. He claimed to have killed 50 deer in 4 years and trapped the same number of bears, 11 foxes and 27 wildcats. On 15 Oct 1890, he reported killing a deer that weighed 300 pounds dressed and once killed a hundred pound lynx. He apparently left the family to wander westward and never returned. When he married for the third time to Mrs. E. J. Hall in OR, he told everyone his first wife had died 8 years earlier and he didn't mention he'd also married a second time but had never divorced either of those women. Actually, his first wife Charlotte was very much alive in Neillsville, WI, struggling to make ends meet and support their large family. William's heart warming story of Abe Lincoln taking him upon his knee and calling him "his little boy soldier" also raised some eyebrows since he'd joined the army at age 23 and the two men were only 13 years apart in age! William died 12 Nov 1912 in Elgin, Union Co., OR, and was buried 14 Nov 1912 in the Elgin City Cemetery. Charlotte was laid to rest after a very hard life 17 Oct 1917 and was buried in the Neillsville City Cemetery along with many of her children and their wives. She was deeply loved and greatly respected her devotion to their family.

Curtis MARKHAM 1822 – 1908 ☆ 🏳

Aka: Amasa Curtis

VGR#176, 25 March 1937, Next of kin: Mrs. Dean Wallis and Mrs. Art Sischo (g-daughters)

Curtis was born in Oneida Co, NY, 2 Feb 1822, the son of Curtis and Sallie Markham. His father died when Curtis was 18 mos. old and, desiring to keep his father's name in the family, the boy's name was changed from Amasa to Curtis. Taken in by his grandfather Samuel Markham, Curtis lived there until the old man's death separated them. His mother had married again, and moved to PA. Curtis had but one brother, Morris (18 Dec 1823) by his mother's first marriage. Curtis married Sarah in Wayne Co, NY, 1 June 1845. She was born in Perinton, NY, 19 Nov 1823, the daughter of Edward Mitchell.

Their daughter Sarah Anna (1850, m. 1871, George Morris; m. 2nd 1878, Wm. McMullen) arrived just before the young family left for Thornton, IL. A few weeks later, they settled in Liberty, Porter Co., IN, where the rest of their children were born: Harriet Adelia (1853, m. Wm. Langley of Lake Co., IN), Julia P. (1856), Ann (1860-1865), John (1863-1864), and Amasa Curtis (1867). Toward the end of the Civil War, Curtis enlisted with Co. A, 35th Indiana Inf. Reg., 13 Jan 1865. He was assigned to the Pontoon Bridge Brigade, but was hospitalized after becoming sick and then detailed as a nurse. Pvt. Markham was discharged 30 Sept 1865. During the early spring of 1868 the Markhams began a new life in Clark Co., WI. The following year they moved to their farm of 80 acres which was split between sec. 17 & 20 in Warner Twp. In 1875 Curtis' brother Morris homesteaded the adjacent farm and their property abutted in sec. 17 but their homes were on opposite sides of the road. Morris' daughter, Julia married Emanuel, the son of Rev. George and Patsy (Burges) Lewis. He was an African-American born in Uniontown, AL, 10 May 1861. Niram H. Withee of Neillsville brought the 5 yr. old boy to Clark Co., WI upon returning from the Civil War and raised him as his own. Emanuel became a lumberman, cultivated a lucrative ginseng business, and farmed in sec. 22 of Warner Twp. He and Julia raised a large family of their own and also adopted a relative's twin sons, Foss and Nate (1904). These two boys were challenged, but were able to work as laborers on area farms. Sarah Markham died two weeks after Easter, 12 Apr 1891. She was laid to rest in the Greenwood City Cemetery and a tree was planted next to her grave. Five years later, Curtis married Abigail "Abbie" Brownell. During the early spring of 1901 the Greenwood Gleaner reported, "Fire destroyed the house on the Haffner farm north of town Wednesday afternoon, destroying nearly all of the property of Curtiss Markham and family who were living there and working the place. The family with what little stuff was saved moved in with their daughter, Mrs. Langley. A pitiable thing about the fire was the fact that the Seyler dog known as "Snap" refused to leave the burning building and held its position on a chair while it was burned to ashes."

The following year Morris Markham, who sometimes stayed at his brother's home, died just before Christmas, 4 Dec 1902. Curtis and Abbie moved to Joplin, Jasper Co., MO. When his wife passed away on 6 Oct 1905, Harriet Langley moved to Missouri to care for her father.

After his death on 11 Sep 1908 at the Veterans' Home in Leavenworth, KS, she returned to Clark Co., WI. She apparently had his body shipped back to Greenwood, where he was buried in the City Cemetery next to the mother of his children and not far from the grave of his brother. Harriet died in Christie, 13 May 1909.

Veteran's Home in Leavenworth Co., KS

Robert McCALVY 1827 - 1922 ☆
VGR#398 dated 27 Feb 1937; Next of Kin: Mrs. Joe Bass (daughter) of Neillsville, WI

Robert was born 29 Aug 1827 in Co. Tyrone, Ireland, the oldest son of Peter and Mary (Reed) McCalvy who immigrated to the USA shortly after his birth. When he turned thirteen the family settled at Cambridge, MA. A year later, they moved to their homestead near Milwaukee, WI. Apparently testing the Luck of the Irish, Robert joined the great gold-seekers' movement to California, walking the entire way behind a yoke of oxen cross-country from Milwaukee to the Coast. Anna Linda, a daughter of John and Mary (Shutter) Rector, became his bride 14 Jan 1849 in Farmington, WI. She was born 4 Mar 1825 at Albany, NY. The McCalvys had 6 children: Adelia Elizabeth (m. **Andrew Bullard**), George E., Sophronia A., Margaret M., Thomas J., and Albert M. During the Civil War, Robert was a Cpl. for Co. G, 14th Wis. Inf. He had enlisted 12 Sep 1863. Two brothers, Thomas and Albert J., were members of Co. A, 7th Wis. Inf. and both were injured at the Battle of Gettysburg. Thomas died from his wound. Albert recovered and returned to his command only to be killed during the Battle of Petersburg. Robert's regiment captured a large cannon at Shiloh. Afterward their General gave it to the victorious soldiers and it was kept in Madison and transported to their reunions. The McCalvys lived in Fond du Lac Co. after the war. In 1868 they homesteaded 160 acres on the 26 Road in sec. 25, Eaton Twp., Clark Co., WI. The first two years, their nearest neighbor lived 2 miles away. Robert said, "We used to have a deer once in a while then…didn't have any turkeys. I spent a number of years in the woods. There were not as many dances then as there are now. We had spelling schools instead, between the schools. New Year's Day 1864 was the coldest New Years we ever had. In Greenwood they had to take the mercury up into a cupola in order to give it a chance to drop. The old Christmases were a great deal better than they are now. They could all be bundled into a wagon on a little straw and with a yoke of oxen could go about to a party. They were more sociable. The presents we used to get were useful. There were no toys about them." He became a member of the Odd Fellows in 1881. In August 1889, he met many of his old war comrades at a reunion in Milwaukee. Robert was among the founding members of the John A. Eaton G.A.R. Post #213. In 1897, he helped construct the Rutger's (Presbyterian) Chapel in his section. He generously gave both time and money to it. At retirement they moved to Neillsville where they lived twenty years. Robert was a charter member of the Charles G. Bacon G.A.R. Even as Robert aged, he was remarkably strong and rarely sick, but during his last 5 years, his health declined. As a 90 yr. old widower he was admitted to the Wisconsin Veterans' Home in Waupaca, 13 Nov, 1917. He was briefly discharged 20 Apr 1918, but readmitted 16 Oct 1922 and died there 5 days later. He was buried in the Neillsville, WI City Cemetery next to his beloved Ann who had passed away 23 Sep 1905.

John A. McCARTY 1847 - 1927 ☆ ⚑

VGR#175 dated 27 Feb 1937, Next of kin: Alvin M. McCarty of Owen, WI (son)

John was born in Luzern Co, PA, 18 Dec 1847, the son of Dominic McCarty (12 May 1798, Loch Erin, Ireland) and Matilda Macloren (1815, Canada). The McCarty's moved to a La Crosse Co, WI farm in the spring of 1857. During the Civil War John enlisted with Co. C, 49th Wis. Vol. Inf., 8 Feb 1865. Pvt. McCarty was honorably discharged 1 Nov 1865. Afterward he settled in Melrose, Jackson Co., WI where he farmed 2 yrs., and in the fall of 1867 moved to Clark Co., WI, to work on the **Wm. Mead** farm and in the pineries during the winters. In the summer of 1872, he acquired his own farm of 200 acres. He was a member of the I.O.O.F. at Greenwood, and also the John A. Eaton, G.A.R. Post #213.

"ANOTHER OLD SOLDIER PASSES AWAY"

The community was saddened by the sudden and unexpected death of J. A. McCarty. Last we mentioned that Mr. McCarty was one of the only remaining old soldiers to survive in the county. On Tue he had been in Greenwood to attend the funeral of his comrade, J. H. Christmas and on Wed. he suffered a stroke which ended his earthly career, death coming on Sun 19 Jun 1927. Funeral services were held from the M. E. Church, burial in the Greenwood cemetery. Mr. McCarty was the first Postmaster at Longwood, having been appointed in Jan 1874, by U.S. Grant, which office he held until 1876, when he resigned. He was also the first Town Clerk of Hixon and he held the office from 1875 to 1886, was Assessor two years, Chairman of the Town Board one year, Constable one year, Justice of the Peace three years, Clerk of School Board six years, School Director three years, and four years as school treasurer, and also filled the office of Treasurer by appointment one year. Mr. McCarty was married 1 January 1872, to Jeanette Smith daughter of Christopher Smith, and they have three children: Almon H., Haskell and Dora E. *Greenwood Gleaner Obituary, 23 Jun 1927.*

*McCarty School: sec. 27, Longwood Twp. 1880 Plat map indicates a schoolhouse was once located there. It is on the property of John McCarty who built the largest log house in Clark County, WI. It was also used as a hotel and was possibly mistaken for a school by the early mapmaker.

John McCarty, of Longwood, is in town being examined by pension examining surgeon Dr. McCutcheon. *The Clark Republican and Press, 11 Feb 1886*

William Henry Harrison MEAD 1833-1911 ☆ ⚐

William & Julia Mead

"Harry" was born in Dutchess Co, NY, 19 Nov 1833, the son of Van Renslear and Margaret (Marshall) Mead, both natives of NY. In 1845 the family settled in Watertown Twp., Jefferson Co, WI. William was married 4 July 1861 to Julia A. Smith, who was born in Herkimer Co, NY, 26 May 1842. She was the daughter of Christopher and Betsy (Pedricks) Smith who'd moved with her family to Jefferson Co. in 1851. During the last year of the Civil War Harry was in the US service putting up telegraph lines in WV. After his discharge the Meads, with two young children in tow, headed for the woodlands of Clark County traveling first by rail to Sparta. There began their overland voyage by wagon over rough roads in wild country. Two days later they reached a cluster of 5 houses, the fledgling community of Neillsville. Greenwood did not yet exist and in its place was a one solitary home surrounded by a dense forest of pine and hardwood. It was owned by Steven and Charlotte Honeywell who provided the Meads with their first night's lodging at the end of their journey. The next day the newcomers started housekeeping ½ mi. away in a shack abandoned by the Dwyers. In the spring of 1866, they homesteaded 6 mi. north of the Honeywells, living in a log shanty, built without a single nail. The snow was 3' deep and the only clearing circled their hand hewn home. Julia soon began feeding travelers, furnishing them with tents to sleep in, while they logged and stumped their land. In 1871, they built a new house and remained on their farm until 1893. Their supplies were purchased at Black River Falls and for the most part, William carried them home on his back. During their first 7 months, only one other white woman came their way. They chained their dog by the door to watch the children whenever they left the cabin to round up their only cow and calf. For three years the Indians were their only close neighbors. In those early days they carried their mail on horseback 2 miles south of the Honeywells to George Huntzicker's hotel, a mile south of where Longwood is today. Julia said they'd hitch up their oxen, drive to Huntzickers and dance until broad daylight, to music furnished by one fiddler, Tom Syth. She'd wear her best dress, taken from the back of their sheep by her own hand when she lived in Jefferson County. Eventually the Meads owned nearly 2,000 acres and logged extensively on both the Black and Chippewa Rivers. Their children were: Frank A., Clara, Helen, Harry, Angus Philo, and Hugh. For seven years William was chairman of the Town Board and chairman of the County Board for two years. He belonged to the Masons, Odd Fellows and the A O.U.W. lodges. He was generous to a fault, never refusing to help anyone in need. When William died 6 Mar 1911, his remains were laid to rest in the Greenwood Cemetery. Julia was also buried there after passing away 18 Aug 1918. Some of the proceeds from this book will be used for the placement of a marker on this veteran's grave.

*See John Blecha's property Map.

"The Dirty Shirt Farm" about 6 mi. N. of Greenwood, along Hwy. 73 was the pioneer home of Harry & Julia Mead. Since her husband had a weakness for poker, she compensated by making a business of laundering clothes for area loggers, and used her earnings to buy their farm. By 1873, the turnpike had been extended from Neillsville to the Mead farm.

George MEEK 1830 - 1897 ☆ 🏳
VGR#177 dated 27 Feb 1937, Next of kin: Sarah Jane Meek (his widow)

George was born 3 Apr 1830, in Macomb Co, MI, the son of Andrew and Margaret Meek, the former a native of PA, and the latter of OH. George's siblings were: George, John, Kate, Alexander and J. Thomas. George moved with his family to a farm in Rock Co., WI, in 1837, remaining there until 1846. They then located in Green Co., before moving to Jackson Co., in 1851, for a short stay prior to settling in Trempealeau Valley where his father died in Apr 1871. George enlisted with Co. "I" in the 14th Wis., Inf. on 29 Oct 1861 serving as a Private and was discharged 30 Jan 1865. He was in the battle of Shiloh. On account of disability, he was on detached duty mostly as cook in a hospital. In later years he drew a pension of $10 pr. month. He married Sarah Jane Harmer 30 Sep 1866. She was born 5 Feb 1849 in Rosedale, the daughter of Charles Harmer of Albion, Jackson Co., WI. George's mother passed away at Black River Falls in Aug 1881. Seven years later, the Meeks moved to Greenwood where George was the mail contractor and stageman between there and Withee. Their children were: Charles H., Hattie A., Hugh and Ralph. George was a member of the G.A.R. Post, and politically was a Republican. George died 28 Apr 1897 and was buried in the Greenwood, WI City Cemetery. Sarah passed away 27 Mar 1897 in the Veterans' Home at Waupaca. Her remains were then buried next to her husband's.

Calvin John MILLS 1843 - 1905
1885 Special WI Veterans' Census

Calvin was born at Medina, OH, June 6, 1843, the son of Peter and Grizelda (Batterson) Mills. At the age of 15 he came to Wisconsin with his grandparents, Jedediah and Mabel (Barnes) Mills. At the first call for troops during the Civil War, Calvin enlisted as a Pvt. with

Co E, 6th Wis. Inf. and served until the close of the war. Charlotte (Raymond) Ransom became his wife in 1866 and they located in Clark County. She was born 30 Jul 1840, in Manlius, Onondaga Co., NY, the daughter of Luther and Julia Ann (Loomis) Raymond. As a youth, Calvin was a member of the Baptist Church, but in 1889 joined the Christie Methodist Church. He attended the reunion of Clark Co. Civil War Soldiers in Neillsville, 3 Jul 1903. Calvin died 29 Jan 1905 and is buried in the Neillsville, WI City Cemetery. After Charlotte passed away in Christie, WI, 24 Oct 1907, she was laid to rest at his side.

August NAGEL 1840 – 1904 ☆
1885 & 1895 Special WI Veterans Census, Loyal

August Nagel was born 27 Aug 1838, in Ger., the son of Heinrich and Wilhelmine (Fittmeier) Nagel. He immigrated to the USA in 1858 and like so many German Immigrants, located in Sheboygan, WI. August enlisted in the Union Army 15 Nov 1862 as a Private with Co. D, 34th Wis. Inf. He served 9 months before being mustered out 8 Sep 1863 at Camp Washburn, Milwaukee, WI. He later filed for an invalid's pension, 15 Jul 1881. After the war he married Caroline Losburger (1850) of Austria. At the time the 1870 Census was recorded, the Nagels were living in the 3rd Ward of Green Bay, WI, and had 2 children: Caroline Clara (1868, m. Sidney McNeill, 4 Jul 1884); and George R. (1870). During 1880, the family moved to Greenwood, sec. 12-13 of Beaver Twp. They worshiped at the Evangelical and Reformed Church in Warner Twp. The other Nagel children were: August (1873), Charles (1873), John (1879), Ernest (3 Jan 1882, d. 24 Apr 1882), Arthur (13 Jul 1883, d. 24 Sep 1883), Willie (9 Jun 1886, d. 12 Jun 1886), and Sidney (2 Apr 1888, d. 4 Nov 1888). That next spring, on 28 Mar 1889, Caroline, the beloved wife and mother died. She was buried in the Greenwood, WI City Cemetery beside her sons: Ernest, Arthur, Willie and Sidney. Henriette (7 Feb 1847), the daughter of Johann and Agolonia (Schell) Muller became August's second wife, 13 May 1890 in Elkhart, WI. That fall, August was granted a homestead claim in sec. 6, Loyal Twp. from the Land Office in Eau Claire. After August died 10 Apr 1904 in Zion City, Lake Co., IL, Henrietta moved in with her daughter Alma and Alma's husband, Frank Dieball in Chicago, IL. She filed for a widow's pension 3 Jul 1914, and passed away in Cook Co., IL on 20 Dec 1939.

Calvin W. NEWTON, Jr. 1847 - 1927
1885 Special WI Veterans Census, Greenwood

Calvin Jr. was born 8 Dec, 1847 in Gaines Twp., Tioga Co., PA, the youngest son of Calvin Sr. and Hannah (Bacon) Newton, who were both natives of NY. At the time of his birth his hard working father was 53 years old and had spent many summer days behind a plow. Like all farmers, the Newton's depended on what they could produce from their land and their surroundings. They had many skills to teach their children and a pioneering spirit that moved them half way across the nation to discover the opportunities of the western lands. By the time the boy had reached his teenage years, the family was living in Stockbridge, WI. He had not yet celebrated his 18th birthday when he joined the Union Army toward the end of the Civil War. Since he was under age his parents' consent was required and they didn't hold him back. He enlisted with Co D, 41st Wis., Inf. as a Pvt. 13 May 1864. After 100 days of duty he was mustered out on 23 Sep 1864. His father did not live to see him marry Mary Anna Smith (9 Jan 1846, Buffalo, NY), 23 Apr 1873. She and Calvin Jr. were the parents of 4 children: Florence May (13 Feb 1873, d. young), Cora Maude (28 Mar 1876, Greenwood, WI, m. #1 William Harry Warner, #2 Frank L. Sifers, d. 1952), LeRoy Cecil (7 Oct 1877, d. 24 Nov 1899, Wadena Co., MN), and Flossie Irene (13 Jan 1884, Clark Co., WI, d. 1910). In the mid 1870's the family moved to Greenwood until that Newton tendency for speculation led them to Wadena Co., MN, before the turn of the century. Even Grandma Hannah Newton went along, but it was her last adventure as she died there in 1896. She surely would have loved to go with Calvin's family when they settled in their last home at Castle Rock, WA. Flossie died in 1910, her mother died in 1921 and Calvin died 18 Apr 1927. They were all buried in Castle Rock, Cowlitz Co., WA.

Milo Lester NICHOLS 1825 – 1897 ☆ ⚐

VGR#156 dated 3 April 1937, "a drifter with no known family" note by John Arends of Greenwood

Milo Lester was born in NY about 1825, the youngest of 9 children of William & Mary "Polly" Nichols. In 1850 his parents were living with him, his wife Cornelia, and sons Philander and Philetus in Summerhill, Crawford Co., PA. By the 1860 Census, this family had fallen apart. Philetus, 11, and Milo Nichols, 6, were living in the poor house in Woodcock, PA. Polly was residing with the family of her daughter Mahala Dodge. Milo seems to have escaped that census, but 1 Sep 1861 while living in Berlin, WI, he enlisted as a Pvt. in the 3rd Wis. Lt. Arty. Bat., under the command of Capt. Lucius H. Drury. His age is given as 44 and he signed with his "✗". Just 2 mo. later, he abandoned his unit at Racine, WI. Like other deserters, he must have had second thoughts about walking away from his duties, because he crossed the Wisconsin border to rejoin at Buckeye, IL, using the alias Lester "Nichles" and falsely stated his age as 28 years.   He was accepted as a Pvt. in Co. G, 93rd Ill. Inf. and mustered in at Chicago 13 Oct 1862. He was described as married, 6' tall, with brown hair, fair complexion, and grey eyes. When filing for an invalid pension, he told of being struck upon the back by a large tree limb while going down Yazoo Pass near Vicksburg, MS, in the spring of 1863. He was detailed for special service in the Subsistence Dept. as a butcher 30 Jun 1863, by Gen. Smith. From Nov '63 through Jun '64 he was listed as "sent sick to Nashville Tenn. 13 Nov 1863." A medical record from Jefferson Gen. Hos., Jeffersonville, IN, from 26 Feb '64, recorded his admittance from Taylor Genl. Hos. (Louisville KY), age 30, single, residence Stephenson Co., IL, nearest relative in Cadis, Green Co., WI, (this was the home of his sister, Mary Meacham), with the diagnosis of rheumatism. The Madison Gen. Hos., Madison, IN, for the period 8 Apr-25 Jul '64 declares him cured of "enzsipelas", with the comment: "He is in good condition, but a malingerer of the first magnitude." He is "Present" on Co. rolls for several months before being "sent sick" to Chattanooga 1 Nov '64, where he remained until he was mustered out 22 June 1865 at De Camp Gen Hosp, Davids Island, NY, under a telegraphic order, sent 4 May 1865 from the War Dept. In Decatur, WI, Milo married Tamma Jane, daughter of Elihu and Betsy Fuller, 12 May 1866. She was the widow of Milo's nephew, William R. Meacham, who died at Ft. Jackson, LA, 1 Jul 1864, while serving with Co. D, 1st Wis., H. A. William had joined the war effort at Monroe, WI, 28 Sep 1863. William's mother, Mary (Nichols) Meacham, was a sister of Milo. Their brother Daniel also came to Wisconsin with his family to settle in

Monroe Co. and his son, Edward Nichols, served with Co. C, 36th Wis. Inf. dying 27 Nov 1864 at Salisbury, NC.

By 1870, Milo was a resident of Pine Valley, Twp., WI, and he and Tamma were the parents of 2 sons, William (1867) and Lester (1869). Milo was issued a 160-acre homestead claim 1 Oct 1874 at the Eau Claire, WI Land Office for sec 24, in the woodland of Weston Twp. West (now Seif). It was nearly 2 years before they had any close neighbors and that spot was filled by Andrew J. Bullard who was also a veteran of the Civil War. By 1880 the Nichols had 4 more children: Jennie (1871), Myron (1873), Fannie (1874) and Frank George (1877).

Milo's behavior became increasingly erratic and Tamma divorced him 17 Mar 1882 at Neillsville. He was admitted to an asylum, probably because he attempted to burn down his family home in Aug 1883. When he escaped Sept 1885, he again threatened his family and his stepson (and grand-nephew) George Meacham took a bullet while attempting to subdue him. Milo was living in Melrose, Jackson Co., WI, at the time of the 1890 Veterans Census. On July 19th of that same year, he was awarded a pension of $12 per mo. for "Injury of right shoulder, rheumatism and disease of heart". At 70 yrs of age, he looked at least 10 years older. He still had a large frame but had lost an inch in his height, weighed 175 lbs. and had a perfectly white full beard and snow white hair. The physician doing the exam looked for proof of Milo's claim that he "rec'd a shot to right shoulder from rifle ball which was never taken out" which crippled his right arm. A scar and a hard, tender enlargement on the right side of the neck seemed to be a possible lodging place of the ball, and there was evidence the muscles in the shoulder, arm and hand had wasted. There was atrophy of muscles of the back, left hip and thigh. It was the doctor's opinion that Milo was entitled to a 12/18 rating for the disability caused by a gunshot wound to the right shoulder and 3rd Grade Rheumatism accompanied with disease of the heart, and 8/18 for the ravages of old age.

The 1895 WI Census shows a household of 1 male and 1 female in Burr Oak, La Crosse Co., WI. A family diary dated 23 Jan 1896, notes; "Milo Nichols & wife here" and on 25 Jan 1896, "Milos went away". There is a marriage record dated 9 May 1892 in La Crosse, WI, for a "Leister Nichols" and Lillie A. Thorp. She may have been Milo's 3rd wife. A request for increase in pension dated 16 Dec 1896 states, "being a poor man, unable to afford the luxury of a nurse, his wife acts in that capacity" and described muscle atrophy, palsy of the extremities, and frequent attacks of syncope due to his heart condition. Milo died 9 Mar 1897 at Cataract, WI, and was buried in the Greenwood, WI City Cemetery with a simple government marker.

William E. OELIG 1840 - 1917 ☆ ⚑
VGR#178 dated 27 Feb 1937, Next of kin: Fred Oelig of New Auburn, WI

William Oelig

William was born 6 Apr 1840 in Canada and came to the United States with his family at the age of nine. His parents, Phillip and Hannah Oelig, were issued a homestead at the Green Bay Land Office 1 Aug 1849 for Fond du Lac Co., WI. The Oeligs and their neighbor,

Gerhard Volkerts, were the first Germans to settle in Auburn. William married Ellen Maria Tuttle (10 Oct 1843, Granville, OH), 4 May 1863. She was born 10 Oct 1843, and moved to the area with her parents Rensselaer and Clarissa (Crozier) Tuttle.

William enlisted with Co. G 14th Wis. Inf., 18 Nov 1863. He was 23 yrs. old and Ellen had just celebrated her 20th birthday. Her two brothers, John "Wesley" and **Albert Tuttle,** also joined the effort the following year. While William was away Ellen gave birth to their daughter Eva Montella at Greenleaf, Brown Co., WI, 19 Jul 1864. Greenleaf was not much more than a railroad stop on the edge of a lake at Wrightstown. It was later known as Random Lake. Today the area is part of the greater Green Bay metro. More importantly to this new mother, it was also the home of her extended family. Pvt. Oelig was discharged 9 Oct 1865 and returned to his young wife and held his daughter for the first time.

Four years later their son Fred Albert was born (Oct 1869, m. Margaret McNamara). Their 3rd child, William E. (May 1877, m. Ella May Leach) was born and their youngest, Grace M. arrived (25 Jun 1880, m. Frank Norris). Eva married Ralph Parker Ferneau 8 Jul 1883 and shortly afterward the newlyweds and her parents all moved to Greenwood, Clark Co., WI. At that time the town was only a small settlement in a very big woods where William and his sons found steady employment in the sawmill and area farms. Eva, Ralph and their granddaughter Vera lived next door to them on Anderson St. The family worshipped at the Methodist Church and William was an active member of the G.A.R. Ellen died 19 Jun 1913 and he passed away four years later, 16 Nov 1917. Both of them are buried in the Greenwood, WI City Cemetery.

Joseph S. PALMER 1844 - 1918
Assumed Member of John A. Eaton G.A.R. post #213

Joseph was born in Sheboygan Co., WI, in April of 1844, the oldest son of William and Esther Ann Palmer. He moved with his parents to Osceola Twp., Fond du Lac Co. sometime in the 1850s. During the Civil War, he enlisted with Co. I, 1st Wis. Inf., and served from 22 Sept 1861 to 13 Oct 1864. Joseph was on duty in KY, TN and GA. After the war he married Jane, the daughter of Anson Windsor. They lived in Osceola Twp, Fond du Lac Co. until relocating to Clark Co., WI in 1872. Joseph owned a farm in Sec. 9, York Twp., near what is now the intersection of H & K. The school house located at that intersection was originally called the "Palmer School" because it was adjacent to Joseph's farm. It was later re-named the "Lincoln School." Jane's father lived with her brother William and his family on 40 acres directly north of them. These neighboring families were some of the area's first settlers.

The Palmers had 4 children: Perry, Bert Nathan, Levi and Grace. At the time of the 1880 Census they were living in Warner Twp. Joseph operated the Hemlock gristmill built by Niram H. Withee on the Black River. Jane died 14 Apr 1892 and Rev. Jefferson of Greenwood officiated at her funeral. She was buried in the York Center Cemetery. Sophronia Bassett, Joseph's sister-in-law, cared for the Palmer children until he remarried in 1896. The family quickly expanded when Joseph's new wife Julia and her children Carrie and John moved to Hemlock. Joseph drew a pension for his Civil War service and 13 Feb 1906, he and **John Sanford** traveled together to Augusta to appear before the examining board regarding an increase in their monthly allotment. Before the 1910 census was taken, Joseph Palmer sold his farm and moved to his last home in the Charleston Precinct, Kitsap Co., WA, where he worked in a shipyard. He died 8 Dec 1918.

Joseph & Jane Palmer→

John Henry PARKER 1840 - 1892 ☆

1885 Special Veterans Census, Unity
VGR #12 dated 3 Jan 1937, information recorded by Harry T. Ketcham

John was born in NY, 22 Aug 1840, the son of George and Mary Ann Parker, who were both natives of England. During the Civil War, John enlisted with the Union Army, 21 Dec 1863. He first served as a Sgt. with Co. E, 118th NY Inf. That regiment primarily drew its recruits from the counties of Clinton, Essex and Warren, and was initially organized at Plattsburg, NY. John's regiment fought gallantly at the **Second Battle of Cold Harbor** but lost 32 of its soldiers. He also participated in the assaults on Petersburg, Fort Harrison, and the advance on Richmond by the Darbytown road where his company's ranks were fearfully depleted when 111 men were wounded or missing. They then attached to the 2nd brigade, 3d division, 24th corps, and were engaged without loss at the fall of Petersburg. He was transferred to Co. C, 96th NY Inf., 12 Jun 1865 and was mustered out 6 Feb 1866, at City Point, VA. After the war he applied for a pension as an invalid 18 Oct. 1886. His wife, Rosetta "Rose" A., was born in MI, 6 Dec 1856. The family farmed in sec. 13, Beaver Twp., Clark Co., WI. They had 5 children, two of them were: Charles (1877); and Myrtle "Mertie" Jane (21 Aug 1880, m. Thomas Tuttle, 21 Apr 1897, d. 31 Oct 1950). John had cancer of the face and sought medical aid in Iola, but the doctors could not cure him. When he died 15 Sep 1892, the G.A.R. took charge of the funeral and he was buried in sec. 13, lot #8 of the Beaver Twp Cemetery. In 1895 Rose married Andrew Jack Gilligan (1854 - 1930) and they later divorced. Their children were Andrew (1897) and Clarie R. (1900, WI). Rose died 11 Apr 1933 and was buried in the Riverside Cemetery, Withee, WI.

Benson PECK 1823 - 1888 ☆⚐

VGR#179 dated 3 April 1937, Next of kin: A daughter living in a Chicago Insane Asylum

Benson Peck, 1863 ca.

Benson was born in Whitehall, Washington Co., NY during 1823, the son of Seth Peck. He served his country twice during the Civil War. He first enlisted with Co. E, 16th Wis., Inf. and later with Co. G 7th Wis., Inf. He was shot in the neck at Wilderness, VA, May 5, 1864 and was able to return to duty only to be wounded again 6 Feb 1865 at Dabney's Mill. He was shot in the left hand and near the thigh in the back of his right leg muscle. His hand required amputation below his fist knuckles. Although his thumb remained it was inflexible and to compensate, he used the specially designed fork shown below.

Benson married Mary "Jane" Ward (ca. 1831, PA) in Jefferson Co, WI, 29 Dec 1848. Sixty-five million feet of logs were being sawed annually for shipping down the Yellow River into the Wisconsin River and on to Galena, IL, to be sold for $11 per thousand feet. Nearly every laborer worked at the Sawmill and Benson was no exception. He and Jane had 2 children: Ella Ann (Nov 1855, WI, m. John Bishop Rose-div., 2nd, m. Ernest Derby) and Hugh Benson (ca. 1873 Lincoln Twp., Wood Co., WI, d. 22 Feb 1888). At the age of nine Hugh was severely wounded by accidentally shooting himself. Later that year, his mother was frightened to death by a bear while picking berries in the woods near their home. Hearing footsteps, she turned to see a huge black bear coming toward her. Dropping her berries, she ran some distance before fainting and falling over a pine log. After regaining her senses she saw the bear quietly eating her berries and managed to slip away. The shock was so profound that after several days of illness, she gradually sank and died 21 Sep 1882, failing to celebrate a 52nd birthday. Benson died 10 Mar 1888 and his marker was ordered from Sheldon & Sons, West Rutland, VT on 21 Aug 1888. Both he and Hugh are buried in the Greenwood, WI City Cemetery.

"Mrs. Peck visited with B. F. Ketchpaw's family last Saturday and Sunday." *Greenwood Gleaner, 16 Feb 1900*

Edwin Thomas PRATT 1838-1917 ☆⚐

"Ed" was born in Bolton, Warren Co., NY, 16 Mar 1838, the son of Thomas and Irinda Pratt. Irinda was a daughter of William and Eunice (Skiff) Hough. Although he was an industrious person, Ed was rather small in stature and only stood 5' 3 1/2" tall when he reached manhood. He had a fair complexion and brown hair and his eyes were blue. At the age of 20 he married 17 yr. old Betsey Ann a week before Christmas, 18 Dec 1858. She had a pleasing nature and made friends easily. Betsey Ann was born in Warrensburg, NY, 18 Apr 1841, the daughter of Nathanial and Angenette Middleton. The Pratts had a farm and also operated a store and livery in Georgetown, NY. Their first baby, Charles H., was born in Dec 1859. Ed enlisted in the Union Army as a harness maker with the 8th NY Cav., 4 Mar 1865 in Lockport. After just a few months service, Pvt. Pratt was mustered out by order of the Secretary of War, 9 May 1865, at Elmira, NY. Therefore, he never actually joined his unit. A son, George F. "Frank" was born that year, and in 1866, a daughter followed, named for Betsey's mother but called "Jennie" by nearly everyone. Hyland "Hiley" (Nov 1873), Minnie (1877), and their youngest, Myrtle (1884), completed the family. After her birth, the family moved to a farm in Weston Twp., Clark Co., WI. "Papa's darling baby" died of diphtheria, 12 Apr 1887 at age 2 yrs, 9 mos. After moving his family to Greenwood in 1888, Ed built a large store and conducted a grocery business. He later sold out to the Klinke Bros. During 1908, he served as Adjutant of the **John A. Eaton Post #213**. His life ended 20 Nov 1917 and he was buried in the Greenwood, WI City Cemetery. His beloved Betsey died 13 Dec 1926, after 9 years of widowhood, and was laid to rest beside him.

"Mrs. E. T. Pratt's brother and sister have been visiting her and returned to their home in New York." *The Clark Republican and Press 18 Aug 1887*

"C.S. Stockwell was up the turnpike doing some surveying this week, and returned early yesterday morning. Ed Pratt, of Greenwood, brought Mr. Stockwell home, receiving for his pay only the honor of riding with the president of the Neillsville Club. We heard Mr. Pratt say that any time Mr. S. wanted to be brought back he had only to call at Mr. Pratt's barn in Greenwood. Ed told a confidential friend yesterday that when he went to his barn to feed his team he found Mr. Stockwell crawling from the hay mow." *Neillsville Republican and Press, 31 Aug 1889*

Mr. and Mrs. E. T. Pratt have been receiving a visit from their daughter, Mrs. J. Covey, of Barron, Wis. She returned home Wednesday." *Greenwood Gleaner 20 Sep 1901*

James RANDALL 1842 - 1908
VGR #13 dated 13 Jan 1937, Inf. by Mrs. Wm. Nelson, Wis. Volunteers

James was born 6 Nov 1842 in Rutland, VT. He was one of the pioneer settlers of Unity, WI, having moved there as a young man. He was a Weston, WI, resident when he enlisted with the Union Army as a Pvt. in Co. B, 17th Wis. Inf. at La Crosse on 11 Oct 1864. He was mustered out 14 Jul 1865 at Louisville, KY. On 20 June 1875 he married Harriett Jane Powers, daughter of Simon & Betsy Powers, at West Salem in La Crosse Co., WI. The couple raised 4 sons: James P., (Jun 1877), Angus R. (Oct 1880), Hugh L. (Feb 1884) and Samuel H. (Aug 1888). Harriett was born 21 Feb 1844 in Canada and moved to Elkhorn, WI, with her parents at the age of 5. She passed away 2 May 1908. Her husband died 7 mos. later on 19 Dec 1908. Both were buried in the Beaver Twp. Cemetery, sec. 13, lot #26.

"The 13-year-old son of James Randall is ill with scarlet fever." *Greenwood Gleaner, 6 Oct 1904 Greenwood Gleaner, 1904*

Sherman RANSOM 1843 - 1888
VGR #529 dated 15 Mar 1937, Next of kin: Lewis Brown (nephew)

Sherman was born in 1843 to Harmon and Leafy (Tuttle) Ransom in New Haven, Huron, OH. He was a cousin and neighbor of **Albert Tuttle** who was married to his sister, Caroline. Sherman's grandparents lived with Albert's family. Another sister, Maryetta (Mrs. Theodore

Brown, Jr.) also lived nearby in sec. 24, near Cawley Creek, Weston Twp. It is obvious that although Sherman was a bachelor, he was surrounded by many close family members. During the Civil War Sherman and his brother Silas both served with Co. G, 14th Wis. Inf. The soldiers who signed on in Neillsville also belonged to the 14th Wis., but were with Co. I. Sherman signed with his "✗" and claimed to be 19 years old when he enlisted 28 Feb 1865 at Empire, Fond du Lac Co., Sub Dist. #17. Pvt. Ransom stood 5' 7" tall, had gray eyes, brown hair and a dark complexion. Why did he falsely state his age? Had he previously attempted to avoid the draft, hoping the war would end before he had to serve? His enlistment took place just 3 days after his older brother **Silas Ransom** had been arrested for desertion, 18 Jan 1863. Another brother, Bostwick (1834), had also deserted at the same time, but was apparently never apprehended and didn't return home to his wife, Charlotte (Raymond) Ransom. Charlotte later married **Calvin Mills**. Could it be that Sherman agreed to serve in exchange for a lighter sentence for his imprisoned brother whose wife and children needed him? Did he want to restore the family's honor or did he hope to find his missing brother, Bostwick? One must wonder if the Ransoms were conscientious objectors, forced to comply with draft laws and raise arms in battle. The fact that the family could brave the hazards and pioneer trials of carving civilization from a wilderness tells us they were definitely not cowards. Whatever the reason for his involvement, Sherman was honorably discharged 9 Oct 1865 at Mobile, AL. Both he and his older brother Silas lived with their father in Weston Twp. when the 1880 census was taken. We don't know if they ever saw Bostwick again. It is possible given the remoteness of the Weston area that he could have visited his family if he lived through the war. When Sherman died in 1888, his family buried him near Silas in the East Weston Cemetery (now Chapel Hill), Clark Co., WI.

Silas H. RANSOM 1831 - 1882
VGR #416 dated 23 Mar 1937, Next of kin: Lewis Brown (nephew), Christie, WI

Silas was born in 1831 in NY, the son of Harmon and Leafy (Tuttle) Ransom. The family moved from NY to OH, but settled in Wisconsin before the 1860 Census. Silas and his wife, Catherine Amanda (b. 1832, NY), were living in Ashford, Fond du Lac Co., WI, when he enlisted as a Private in Co. G, 14th Inf. Regt. on 1 Jan 1862, along with his brother Bostwick. His brother Sherman served with the same unit from Feb to Oct 1865. On 18 Jan 1863, after a year of service, Silas and Bostwick deserted. Silas was arrested 25 Feb 1865 and court-martialed on 22 May 1865 at Montgomery, AL. He was sentenced to a year of hard labor at Ft. Jefferson, FL, aka "America's Devil's Island." It was reputedly one of the Union Army's worst prisons. However, he escaped custody 11 Jul 1865. His regiment was mustered out 9 Oct 1865 at Mobile, AL. Bostwick never returned to his family in Wisconsin and his wife remarried in 1866. In the 1870 Census, Silas and Catherine were living in Weston, Clark Co., WI, with his widowed father and his brother Sherman. His younger brother William married Floretta, the daughter of **Luther Raymond**. When Catherine passed away 5 Aug 1873, her funeral was held at the Hyslip schoolhouse. Silas suffered a long and severe illness before passing away at the home of his brother on Cawley Creek, 21 Jun 1882. He was buried in sec. 11, lot #34 in the Neillsville, WI City Cemetery next to his wife's grave.

Luther RAYMOND 1809 - 1883

VGR #528 dated 20 Feb 1937, Next of Kin: Claude Mills, Grandson

Luther was born 5 Apr 1809, in Manlius, Onondaga Co., NY, the son of Ebenezer and Eunice (Daniels) Raymond. Julia Ann married Luther 5 Nov 1833. She was born 22 Oct 1817 in NY, the daughter of Philander and Betsey (Tichnor) Loomis. The Raymond children were: Eben Deloss (19 Jul 1834), Charlotte Ann (1 Jul 1840), and Floretta (1847). They first located in Erie Co., NY, and remained there until about 1843. The Raymonds then settled in what is today Waukesha Co., WI. They were pioneer residents when Wisconsin was admitted to the union as the 30th state. A year later, Luther was granted an 80 acre homestead claim of wild land, 1 Aug 1849, by the Land Office in Green Bay, WI, for sec. 12 of Township 14-N, Range 18-E, Fond du Lac Co. With hard work, this property was developed into a productive farm. Julia passed away when she was just 30 years old, 20 May 1863, in Campbellsport, WI. She was buried in the Union Cemetery and not long afterward, Luther enlisted in the Civil War. He served with Co. G, 39th Wis. Inf. after enlisting 28 May 1864 in Sheboygan, WI. He was mustered out 22 Sep 1864. In 1870, he moved with his family to a tract of wild land in Weston Township. When they first arrived, there was only a foot path to their home, and the Indians were numerous in the vicinity. It was a full two years before their family even had a cow. By 1873, Luther was both farming and doing road work services, including "chopping" along with **Charles Kayhart**, **Jacob Demouth** and Loren Gates. After being a widower for over 20 years, Luther died 15 Dec 1883, and was buried in the East Weston Cemetery (now Chapel Hill).

James C. REDWINE 1838 - 1925

1885 (Withee) & 1895 Special WI Veterans' Census (Greenwood)

James was born 1 Sep 1838 in Logansport, IN the 2nd son of Frederick (1803, VA) and Elizabeth W. (Roush) Redwine. They married 21 Dec 1837 in Marion, IN. Frederick was a mill digger and in 1850 their family was living in Tippecanoe, IN. His mother died when James was 15 years old (4 Dec 1810-30 Jan 1853). James married three times, first to Fatha "Lucy" Ellen Sellers in Frankfort, IN, 17 Jun 1860. He and Lucy had a son, John Henry Elden (1 Jun 1860, Frankfort, IN). Later that summer, James was enlisted in Co. H, 86th Ind. Inf., 14 Aug 1862 by Capt. Bell for a 3 yr. term. Pvt. Redwine's military records indicate he was a resident of Middle Fork, IN at that time. He stood 5' 11" tall and had blue eyes, brown hair, and a light complexion. Two months later he deserted his regiment near Crab Orchard, KY, 16 Oct 1862. The family story is that he left his unit after being wounded during a battle at "Pea Hill" [Pea Ridge?]. Following the war his daughter Rosetta (8 Apr 1866, Frankfort, IN) was born. In 1878 James married 16 yr. old Nancy Ann (4 May 1862) in Washington Co., WI. A few months later their son Frederick (4 Mar 1878, WI, named for his grandfather) was born. Nancy was the daughter of George and Elizabeth (Smith) Miller. The Redwines, including James' son, 21 yr. old John Henry, Frederick and their 3 mo. old daughter Lilly (23 Mar 1880, MO), were living with Nancy's family in Lewis, MO, in 1880. Three years later they were living in KS, where their son William was born (24 Mar 1883). The following year James Jr. (29 Aug 1884) was born. James was farming in Longwood, WI, at the time of the 1885 census and was resident of Greenwood when the 1895 census was taken. His son John Henry rented a farm in Warner Twp. He'd married Abbie Julia, 9 Sep

1885. She was the daughter of **John Asa and Mary Ann (Olson) Scovil** of Beaver Twp. The other children of James and Nancy were: George Albert (14 Jan 1887, Clark Co, WI, m. Lizzie Griesbach), Luella (10 Mar 1889 in Clark Co., WI), Nora (29 Jun 1892), Roy (29 Oct 1895 in Cleveland, Taylor, WI), and Ruby (29 Oct 1895, a twin of Roy). Nancy married Lewis T. Wood on Christmas Day, 1906. The third wife of James was Sarah A. Harrison (1829, Parke Co., IN). He died 1 Sep 1925 in Winnebago, WI, and is buried at Riverside Cemetery, Ladysmith, WI, where he resided near his son and daughter.

Joseph RENSIMER 1830 – 1914 ☆
1875 Census-Beaver Twp., Clark Co., WI & 1890 Special WI Veterans' Census

Joseph was born 28 Feb 1830 in Lehigh Co., PA, the son of Jacob Sr. and Rebecca (Snyder) Rensimer. He helped his parents to clear two Ohio farms and learned the hatter's trade. Barbara Ebinger became his wife in Worchester, OH, 3 Oct 1851. She was born 7 Jul 1829, in Württemberg, Germany. In 1852 they moved to a Michigan farm, where Joseph also worked at his trade. Because of failing health, the Rensimers returned to the Buckeye state to live in Lafayette. In 1861, they went to Christian Co., IL, and then to Columbia Co., WI. At Pardeeville, WI, Joseph enlisted with Co. A, 37th Wis. Inf. and served as a Cpl. until 1865–1 yr., 3 mo., 15 days. Upon his return to civilian life, he did wagon making. He acquired an 80 acre homestead in sec. 2, Beaver Twp., Clark Co, WI, 20 Nov 1875. Their only neighbors were Henry G. Smith to the west and John Allen to the east. The next year, Sam Clark, Henry Twing and **Chester Burgess** moved to that neck of the woods and in 1878 David Cummings arrived. When O. B. Matteson moved there in 1882, their tiny farm community was complete. Together they tackled the tremendous task of clearing the timber and brush to expose enough earth to cultivate a life-sustaining garden for each family. They also built cabins for protection from the prowling animals and the freezing temperatures. The Rensimer children were: Mary (1853, m. Geo. W. Peterson), John E. (1854, m. 1st Lillie Stewart, 2nd Hannah Stewart), Margaret "Maggie" C. (1857, m. Emil McMiller), Corwin "Calvin" (1860, m. Edith Romaine), Florence E. (1862, m. Leonard Barber) and Carrie E. (1866, m. Frank Salter). Joseph was a member of the Town Board, held school offices, was treasurer of the I.O.O.F. and Sgt. of the Unity Guards. By 1880 their property had been sold to N. Horner and they'd moved to the east side of Colby, WI. Later the Rensimers became residents at the King Veteran's Home 8 Jul 1903 from Prentice, WI. Jacob died there 24 Feb 1914. Barbara had been discharged from the home 26 Jul 1908 and then readmitted 11 Aug 1912. She died in 1934, at the age of 105 after 20 years of widowhood and is buried in the Central WI Veteran's Memorial Cemetery next to Jacob.

Charles "Carl" RICHELIEU 1838 – 1917 ☆ ⚑
VGR#180 dated 27 Feb 1937, Next of kin: Chris Richelieu of Owen (Son), 1890 Special WI Veterans Census

Carl was born 15 Sept 1838, near Trondjhem, Norway, the son of Carl N. and Christina Richelieu. In 1861, he came to the USA, settling in Springfield Township, Jackson Co., WI. He engaged in lumbering during the winter months, and farming in the summer. During the Civil War draft, Carl was not assigned to a Regiment when he enlisted 18 Nov 1863, but served as a Pvt. until he was discharged 13 Jan 1864, due to sickness. He moved to Clark Co., WI in 1871, settling on his farm in sec 36, Warner Twp., which was at that time covered with heavy timber. He owned 120 acres with 70 acres cleared, where he farmed and raised livestock. In Feb 1862, Carl married Christina Marie, daughter of Christian Christensen. She was born 29 Jan 1836 in Trondjhem, Norway, and immigrated to Black River Falls, WI, with her parents in 1850.

"...In the early days there was no veterinary here although **Carl Richelieu**, who lived east of town, helped out when needed." *The Hub of Clark County (1853 - 1934)*

The Richelieu's children were: Theodore Martin (24 Jul 1864, m. Ida Steel, d. 1 Jul 1931), Christian C. (12 Apr 1865, m. Gina "Jennie" Severson, d. 21 Feb 1959), Mary Ann (m. Nixon) and Charles. Carl was a member of the Town Board several years, and its Chairman for 1 ½ years. He was the "Road Overseer" 11 years, a member of the School Board several years and acted as the Director for a period of time. The family worshiped at the Lutheran Church. He was an enterprising and public-spirited citizen who voted a Republican ticket. He donated generously to charitable and benevolent purposes. Carl's beloved "Marie" died 8 Jan 1914 and he died 17 Nov 1917. They are both buried in the Greenwood, WI City Cemetery.

"A young lady came to the home of Mr. and Mrs. Chris Richelieu Monday Morning asking to be kept for twenty-one years. Mother and child are doing well." *Greenwood Gleaner, 30 Aug 1901*

"Carl Richelieu has purchased an eighty north of Wm. Stabnow's place, making 120 acres which Mr. Richelieu owns there." *Greenwood Gleaner, 25 Apr 1902*

James Walter ROBBINS 1839 - 1922 ☆
1885 Special WI Veterans' Census

James was born 16 Oct 1839 in Liberty, Licking Co., OH, the 4th of Ira Allen and Mary (Safford) Robbins' 11 children. His siblings were all born in OH: Charles Henry (28 Jun 1834, McKean); Sewell Smith (15 Dec 1835, McKean); Mary (28 Sep 1837, McKean); Zenas Safford (6 Apr 1841, Liberty Twp.); Cynthia Elizabeth (30 Jan 1844, Liberty Twp); Davis Mack (19 Feb 1846, Liberty); Ira Oscar (12 Jan 1848, Johnstown); Joseph Packard (3 Nov 1849, Johnstown); Emma Jane (11 Apr 1852, Newton Twp); and Edwin Rupert (26 Apr 1854, Taylor). Ira was the son of Zenas and Cynthia (Goodenough) Robbins. Zenas was an early settler (1788) of the town of Hancock, Addison Co., VT and built that town's 1st sawmill. Ira was born in Hancock 9 Sep 1807 and was married there 7 Mar 1833 to Mary Safford (1813-1895). Both are buried in Broadway Cemetery, Taylor Twp., Union Co., OH. During the Civil War, James fought as a Pvt. with Co. K, 1st Ohio Cav. He enlisted 1 Oct 1861, was promoted to Full Sergeant 1 Nov 1864, and mustered out 13 Sep 1865 at Hilton Head, SC. He was married 8 Oct 1867 in Hancock, VT. By the 1870 Census he was settled in Weston Twp., Clark Co., WI. James and his wife, Jessie Nelsine "Nellie", were among the first pioneers to live in Christie, settling on a farm in sec. 10 near La Fleur's mound right after the Civil War. She was born 17 Nov 1845 in VT, the daughter of H. N. and Phoebe Bull. Their children were Harry B. (b. 1869, m. Florence Jaseph, d. 1897), Clinton J. (b.

1872) and Mabel H. (b. 1873, m. 1st Richard Boon, d. 1900; m. 2nd H. M. Loomis). Mabel taught school in Weston and after being widowed attended business college at Stevens Point, becoming a stenographer. She also ran a photography studio in Amherst, WI. His wife and daughter remained in WI, but James appears in Chicago in the 1900 Census, in Gerrish, MI, in 1910, and in later years made his home in an Old Soldiers' Colony at Zephyrhills, Florida. His son Clinton moved to Dayton, OH, and it was while visiting his son Harry in Denver, CO that James passed away, 16 Jan 1922. His wife Jessie died 3 Aug 1924 and was buried in Neillsville City Cemetery, near their daughter Mabel and granddaughters Jessie and Ethel.

Old Soldiers' Colony, Zephyrhills, Florida

Frank J. ROFINOT/RUFINOT 1848 – 1895 ca.
1885 Special WI Veterans' Census, Greenwood, 1890 Special OR Veteran's Census, Clatskanie

Frank was born in NY about 1848 to Eugene & Nancy Rofinot, natives of France. His parents were farming in Charlestown, Calumet Co., WI, with Frank and his brother Luther when the 1860 Census was taken. On 22 Feb 1865, he followed his brother into military service, enlisting in Co. E, 22nd Wis. Inf. Reg. He also served in Co. U, 3rd Inf. Reg., and was mustered out 2 Jul 1865. He followed up by serving in the Provisional Permanent Battalion at Camp Randall, Madison, WI.

Camp Randall, Madison, WI

Frank married Elizabeth A. (1851, NY) and by 1870 they had two sons: Edgar Francis (1868) and William E., (Oct 1869, m. Naomi E. & moved to Seattle, WA, to work on the docks). Frank farmed in sec. 27, Eaton Twp., Clark Co., WI, and the 1880 Census shows two more sons: Victor (1871) and George H. (1877). In May 1887 he signed a witness statement regarding fellow soldier **George W. Slater**'s pension as a "resident of La Crosse" and by the time the 1890 Veteran Schedule was taken he was living in Clatskanie Pct., Columbia Co., OR. Frank couldn't be located on the 1900 Census and we assume he died before it was recorded.

Louis ROFINOT/RUFINOT 1841 – 1888 ☆ 🏳
VGR#183 dated 27 Feb 1937

Louis (aka Rufus) was born 1841 in NY to Eugene & Nancy Rofinot, natives of France. He enlisted as a Pvt. with Co. K, 4th Wis. Cav., 24 Apr 1861. He was discharged 2 July 1864, but enlisted in Co. E, 22nd Wis. Inf. serving from 22 Feb 1865 to 24 Jun 1865. He and Sarah Good were married 5 Dec 1866 in Gravesville, Calumet Co., WI, and had three sons before moving to Marquette, MI, where their youngest son was born. Sarah was a native of Ontario, Canada, born of Irish parents who came to Wisconsin about 1856. Their sons were: Henry (1869), Louis (1875, d. 1900, MN), Nelson (21 Apr 1879, d. 22 Aug 1946, WA) and Eugene (25 May 1883, d. 23 Apr 1932, OR). The family returned to WI, settling in Eaton, Clark Co., before 1885. Louis died while at work in the old Farming mill near the family home, 13 Feb 1888, when an emery wheel burst. Sarah Rofinot was only 54 years old when she collapsed and died 9 Aug 1900. When her 15-yr. old son, Eugene, went to telegraph his brothers, a message from the Duluth, MN authorities, informing them that his brother Louis was dead was waiting for him. Another brother, Nelson, had spent the previous winter with Louis, but, because his address was unknown, he was unaware of either the death of his brother or mother, leaving Eugene to bear the double affliction alone. Both Louis and his wife, Sarah, are buried in the Greenwood, WI City Cemetery.

Edward Wells ROMAINE 1840 – 1905 ☆
1885 Special WI Veterans' Census & VGR# 418, dated 3 Apr 1937

Mr. & Mrs. Edward W. Romaine

Edward was born 6 Sep 1840, in Paterson, NJ, the son of Benjamin Ralph and Charity (Hopper) Romaine. At the age of ten, he accompanied his parents to Fond du Lac Co., WI. On Christmas Day 1862, he married Celia M. Roscoe who was a school teacher. She was born 5 Jan 1844 in Milwaukee, the daughter of James T. and Eliza A. (Finch) Roscoe. In 1864, "Ed" enlisted as a Pvt. with Co. C, 14th Wis. Inf. serving until the close of the war. In 1868, the Romaine family became pioneers in Clark Co., WI, being some of the first settlers of Beaver Twp., where they homesteaded 160 acres of heavily timbered land in sec. 36. Persistently determined and energetic, they immediately began erecting a log cabin and stables and clearing land until they found themselves owners of a well-cultivated farm and a new frame home with a complete set of barns and outbuildings. They were the parents of Edith Deyette (30 Jan 1864), Mary E. (Nov 1865), Leah Estella (19 Jun 1871), Jessie I. (21 Sep 1875) and Robert Edward (16 Feb 1878-8 Sep 1881). In 1893, because of Celia's failing health, they moved into the village of Loyal, WI. Ed was an active citizen who served in a variety of public offices, including that of Deputy Sheriff. He was a friendly individual who was always willing to do more than his fair share. In 1905, while on their way to the fair in Portland, OR, they stopped in Idaho to visit with daughter, Mrs. C. M. Ransimer. Shortly after their arrival, Ed became ill and died there two weeks. His remains were returned to Loyal, WI, and then buried in Neillsville. Ed was an honored member of the Hercules Lodge, I.O.O.F., and of the Greenwood G.A.R. post. Edward died 29 Jul 1905 in Coeur d'Alene, ID. Celia passed away 26 Apr 1924 in Inglewood, CA, and was buried in Neillsville.

Jacob Lewis ROOHR 1847 - 1921 ☆

1885 Special WI Veterans' Census

Jacob was born in Springfield Twp., Mahoning Co., OH, 20 Dec 1847, son of George Christian and Margaret Ann (Sisnault) Roohr. The family moved to Wisconsin where his father served as a corporal in the Civil War with Co. I, 27th Wis. Inf. After completing his 9 month term, he enlisted for an additional three years. He died in 1866, shortly after returning home. Jacob followed in his footsteps and enlisted at Fond du Lac, serving with Co. D, 45th Wis. Inf. under General Thomas at Nashville. Toward the end of the war, during July of 1865, he was injured in a train wreck. After returning to civilian life, he worked five years with the Monroe Brothers' sawmill at Green Bay. He then farmed in Washington Co. for a year before moving to Neillsville. For a couple of years he worked as a farmhand and also did millwork in Beaver Twp. He married Gertrude Ann in Swamico, WI, 6 May 1873. She was born 19 Jul 1855 in Milwaukee, the daughter of John and Mary Ann (Gross) Steele. As a 5 yr. old, she'd moved with her parents to Duck Creek. The Roohrs had 10 children: George Christian (1 Nov 1874, m. Alma Sumner), Mary Ann (13 May 1875, m. Ernest Stowe of Beaver), William Archie (25 Dec 1876, m. Lisey Rake), Margaret "Maggie" (Sep 1878, m. Geo. Sumner of Beaver), Frederick C. (17 Jul 1882, m. Clara Wisnaskye), Jacob Henry (21 Oct 1885, m. Stellie Stringem), Anna (Jul 1891), Nettie P. (6 Sep 1893, m. Thomas Plumstead), John Lewis (5 May 1896) and Hazel Sansen G. (Dec 1897, m. Vernon Goutcher). At first Jacob supported his family by cutting maple wood and exchanging it for 75¢ worth of groceries per cord. Occasionally he'd drive a yoke of steers from Neillsville to Hewettville to have corn ground into meal. Later the Neillsville lawyer, Clarion A. Youmans, hired him to manage his 400-acre stock farm on Pleasant Ridge, including one of the finest herds of registered Holstein cattle in the county. About 1903 Jacob bought 120 acres of heavily timbered land from B. Curtis of Columbia Co., WI. He had to chop a trail to the property because there were no roads in the vicinity. Beginning with 6 head of horned cattle and 4 horses, he expanded his stock with quality Durham, Guernsey and Pole cattle. He also built a good barn and a nice home. The family worshiped at the Methodist Church and Jacob belonged to the G.A.R. and the Guardians of Liberty. When his health began to fail, they purchased a home in Loyal, WI, and after a year-long illness he died Tuesday, 14 Jun 1921, at the age of 72. His funeral was held at the Modern Woodman of America Hall and he was laid to rest in the Loyal City Cemetery. Gertrude passed away in Greenwood seven years later, 11 Dec 1928, and was buried next to Jacob.

Charles ROSEMAN 1829 – 1921 ☆
1885 Special WI Veterans' Census, Weston Twp., Clark Co.

"Carl" was born 8 Apr 1829 in Silesia, Germany. He fought with Co. B, 19th Wis. Inf. entering the service 24 Feb 1862. He was wounded at Fair Oaks, VA, 27 Oct 1864 and received an honorable discharge in the heat of summer, 9 Aug 1865. His first marriage to Eliza Gothe ended in divorce 30 Oct 1871 and she died in 1893. Albert J. Roseman (b. 9 Oct 1867, Racine, WI, d. 30 Aug 1933, Marshfield, WI) was Carl's son by this first marriage. The family story is that his mother, who was living in Sparta, was not caring for him properly and in 1871 Carl snatched him and moved nearly a hundred miles away to the woods of Clark Co., WI. Carl's second wife, Sophia Anna Maria Behrens, was born 9 Sep 1833 in Beidendorf, Mecklenburg, Ger., Province of Slagen, Prussia, the daughter of John J. & Elizabet Dorothea (Hameister) Kneiser. She and Carl married in Neillsville, WI, 12 Aug 1876. They moved to sec. 3, Weston Twp., Clark Co., WI, in 1879 along with his 76 yr. old mother-in-law. Sophia's children by her first marriage to Fred Behrens were: Frederick J., John H., Josephine "Josie", Otto, Georgena Johanna Mayta, William Gene, and Alexander Ayres, who was born out of wedlock to "Josie" Behrens, but raised as her brother. In later years, Georgia remembered living in their large home in Milwaukee before her parents divorced in 1872. Her mother would apparently sprinkle gold dust in her hair to make it sparkle before driving off to parties with their horse and carriage. Albert left home at the age of 14 to cook for the performers on the circus trains, a career that took him all over the USA and even into Canada, Cuba and the Bahamas. He married Louise Profilio 27 Jun 1900. Carl and Sophie were admitted to the WI Veterans' Home in Waupaca from Neillsville, 17 Aug 1918. Carl died there 20 Apr 1921 and Sophia passed away the following year, 13 Oct 1922. They were both buried in the Central WI Veterans' Memorial Cemetery in graves 23 & 24, sec. 3, Lot 37.

Paul George ROSSMAN 1842 - 1918 ☆ 🏳
VGR#182 dated 25 March 1937; Next of Kin: Roy Rossman (grandson) of Rt. 1, Withee, WI

Paul was born in Neirstein, Ger., 16 Mar 1842, the son of Ludwig and Louisa Catharina (Ebling) Rossman who immigrated to Plymouth, Sheboygan, WI in 1851. He enlisted as a Pvt. with Co. A, 9th Wis. Inf., 14 Sept 1861. He was mustered in at Camp Seigel, Milwaukee on 18 Nov. His regiment was assigned to the 1st Army Brigade of the 3rd Div. He fought at Newtonia, Prairie Grove, Spoonville, Little Missouri River, Prairie De Ann, Poison Springs, Camden Road, and Jenkin's Ferry. He held the rank of Cpl. when he mustered out 3 Dec

1864. The following year he married Joanna, the 19 yr. old daughter of Henry and Margaret (Schmutzler) Russler, 12 Apr 1865. "Anna" was born 10 Mar 1846 in Bavaria, Germany, and when she was 7 years old, her family immigrated to St. Louis, MO. Paul was a blacksmith there when she became his wife.

In 1884 the Rossmans moved to Clark Co, WI, to farm 7 mi. east of Greenwood. Their children were: Louis Alfred (d. young), Alfred L. (of Priest River, ID), Elisabeth Catharine (20 Jan 1868), Lilly Emma (12 Sep 1869, m. Thomas Cochran, 16 Jun 1886); Paul Robert (2 Jun 1873, m. Helen Lena Humke, 4 Jul 1901), Lydia (m. Geo. Cochran of Bemidji, MN), Tushelda Nelda (29 Sep 1874, m. Henry Nutting), and Olga Francis (10 Jul 1876, m. Arthur E. Darton, 1 Jan 1896). Their nephew, Roy Peter Rossman (Mar 1889), was also raised with the family following his mother's death, just days after his birth. In 1894 the family moved into town.

Paul died the morning of 24 Jan 1918 and his funeral was held with full military rights in the Woodmen Hall. Interment was in the city cemetery with the Odd Fellows in charge of the burial. Anna passed away at the home of her daughter Lydia 3 May 1921. Her funeral service was held in Greenwood and she was laid to rest next to her husband.

"Mr. and Mrs. Paul Rossman returned Monday evening from an extended visit with old friends and relatives in Sheboygan County and report a most enjoyable trip. This was the first in twenty years and while they found many improvements and changes they found a most cordial reception wherever they went." *Greenwood Gleaner, 13 Aug 1904*

"Paul Rossman had a well dug on his property on Harrison Street." *Greenwood Gleaner, 12 Aug 1909-- 18 yrs ago.*

Phillip ROSSMAN 1836 - 1891 ☆ ⚑

1885 Special Veterans' Census, VGR#181, 3 Apr 1937, Next of kin: Roy Rossman of Withee (Grandson)

Phillip was born in Hesse Darmstadt, Ger., 4 Mar 1836, the son of Ludwig and Johann Rossman. He immigrated to Sheboygan Co., WI with his parents in 1851, where he was a carpenter and woodsman. After 1855 he followed at his trades in TN, MO, and IA. Then in 1859, he met Angeline Mary Dohogne of France (2 Feb 1840) and became a married man. She'd come to America with her parents to Cape Girardeau, MO. Her sister was already living in Sheboygan Co., WI. When the Civil War was pending, Phillip was forced to return to the north. His son Adolph reported that his father served in a Wisconsin Co. in the Civil War. Phillip served under the Quartermaster in the 1st Brigade during the Battle of Nashville.

That was James Lowry Donaldson, who was a Brigadier General and Chief Quartermaster of the Military Division of Tennessee who managed the armies of Ulysses S. Grant and William T. Sherman. This unit received high commendations in official reports At the close of the war, Donaldson was promoted to Major General.After the war Phillip returned to Sheboygan Co. and remained there until he built a sawmill in Beaver Twp., Clark Co., WI, during 1871. The area was sparsely settled with neighborhoods of 2-4 families from 3-4 mi. apart in the dense forest with only small cleared patches around their log cabins. It was like one enormous deer park. There were tens of thousands of them available to hungry pioneers and there were no game wardens protecting any of the wildlife. Keeping the deer from the Rossman's garden was a 24 hr. a day task, but they never wanted for fresh meat or dried venison. Sometimes droves of a hundred or more deer would graze in small clearings. Bears, panthers and wildcats were frequent nighttime visitors and the howl of the wolves filled the air in the light of the moon. The brooks were so shaded that only speckles of sunshine could reach them. This is where Phillip attempted to farm and handled an extensive lumber business. He was a friendly man who held several town offices, and represented Beaver Twp. on the County Board for several years. Elected as a Representative for the Clark Co. district in the WI State Legislature he served until his death. Both the Odd Fellows and G.A.R. were dear to his heart. The Rossman children were: John P. (1860-1930), Adolph Paul (22 May 1862-11 Apr 1950), Mary (1867-1967), Edward Fred (1867-20 Feb 1933), Lucy Sophia (17 Mar 1868), Lionel (1869-8 Mar 1912, Zion City, IL), Ira J. (1873), and Elmer J. (17 Nov 1877-1971). Phillip died 7 Dec 1891 at the Emergency Hospital in Chicago, far removed from his country home. Following an operation for cancer of the rectum, his strength did not return. Between eight and nine hundred people attended his funeral. Among them were legislature members including: Senators M. C. Ring, R. J. MacBride, and James O'Neill of Neillsville, Assemblymen J. McGilvery of Black River Falls; and his brother Louis Rossman. Angeline passed away 13 Nov 1923 and both she and Phillip are buried in the Greenwood Cemetery.

"Phillip Rossman left on Saturday for Chicago for medical treatment." *Greenwood Gleaner, 25 Nov 1909--18 yrs ago*

"The large gray team of colts owned by B. F. Thompson and driven by Fred Oelig, which was employed to take the pall bearers to the residence of **Phillip Rossman**, became unmanageable and ran into a buggy occupied by John Stewart and **Robt. McCalvy**. No one was hurt, but considerable damage was done to the Stewart buggy." *Greenwood Gleaner, 9 Dec 1909--18 yrs ago*

"The literary Society met with Angeline Rossman." *Greenwood Gleaner, 2 Dec 1909--15 yrs ago*

"Mrs. Angeline Rossman was on the sick list this week." *Greenwood Gleaner, 18 Dec 1909--15 yrs ago*

John SANFORD 1839 - 1917 ☆
1885 & 1895 Special WI Veterans' Census, Greenwood, Warner Twp.

John was born in Allegany Co., NY, 7 Aug 1839, the son of Zephaniah and Mary Sanford who were both natives of the Empire State. His siblings were: Lemuel (1826, NY), Sarah (1831, NY), Samuel (1832, NY), Esther (1834, NY), Ephraim (1836, NY), James (1841, NY), Sirena (1843, PA), Ira (1846, PA), and Ralph (1848, PA). The family moved to

Shippen, McKean, PA, about 1843 to farm. In 1860 John was 22 years old and living with his older brother Lemuel and sister-in-law Betsey in Norwich, PA, which was served by the Port Allegany Post Office. He served as a Pvt. with Co. I., 76th Penn. Inf., 1 yr. 11 mo., 27 Aug 1863 - 10 Jun 1865. His unit participated in the conflicts at Drewry's Bluff, **2nd Cold Harbor,** (the namesake of the Greenwood G.A.R., **John A. Eaton** died there) Petersburg, Richmond, Fair Oaks, Wilmington and others. After returning to civilian life, John married Louise Swift 9 May 1869, but the 1880 Census indicates he was divorced and living with his brother Ephraim in sec. 29, Warner Twp. An 1893 map shows John's property in sec. 8. He was an active G.A.R. member in Greenwood and was installed as Officer of the Guard, 27 Jan 1906. The next month, he and **Joseph Palmer**, the Hemlock miller, appeared before the pension examining board in Augusta to seek an increase in pension. An uncalled for letter addressed to John Sanford was noted in the 21 Mar 1889 Republican and Press Post Office Notices. The 1905 WI State Census listed him as a widowed boarder, living in Warner Twp. He married Margaret A. Williams in Greenwood 18 Jan 1909. John died in Farmington, Waupaca, WI, 10 Jul 1917 and Margaret later married Alfred Wheeler 25 Jan 1926.

"Frank and Morgan Silvers are clearing for John Sanford. Mr. Sanford talks of building another house this summer to replace the one that was burned down a year ago last winter."
Greenwood Gleaner, 28 Mar 1904

John "Asa" Turner SCOVEL 1842 - 1910 ☆ ⚑
VGR#184 dated 25 March 1937, Next of kin: Ezra Scovel of Ladysmith, WI.

John was born 4 Mar 1842 in Stockton, NY, the son of John T. and Olive (Belden) Scovel. In 1860, "Asa" was living with his parents in Fillmore Co., MN. His father was born in VT and his mother was a native of CT. Asa enlisted with Co. F, 1st Minn. Cav., 6 Nov 1862 at the age of 20 yrs. He served as a Pvt. until he was honorably discharged 20 Dec 1863. His Cavalry Regt. was known as the "Mounted Rangers." His regiment fought in Sibley's Expedition against the Dakota Indians from 16 Jun - Sept 14, 1863.

They then took part in the battle of Big Mound, Dakota Territory, 24 Jul 1863; the Battle of Dead Buffalo Lake, 26 Jul 1863; at Stony Lake, 28 Jul 1863; and engaged in operations along the Missouri River 28-30 Jul 1863. After reorganization at St. Cloud, St. Peters and Fort Snelling, MN, 9 Oct to 30 Dec 1862, they engaged in frontier duty until June 1863, followed by duty at Fort Ripley. The rest of the Reg. was stationed at Fort Snelling, MN, until 7 Dec 1863, when it was mustered out. The unit had lost 2 officers and 4 enlisted men. 31 men were killed or died of battle wounds and another 31 soldiers died of disease. On 17 Nov 1867, John married Mary Ann (9 Oct 1842). At the age of 18, she immigrated from Kragero, Norway, to Spring Valley, MN, with her parents, Knute & Neut Oleson. The Scovels had 5 daughters and 2 sons: Clara Josephine (1869-1911), Abbie Julia (19 Jan 1871, Spring Valley, MN), Anna Asalia (26 Nov 1872, MN), Mary Elizabeth (Jun 1876, MN), John Ezra (21 Feb 1878, Greenwood, WI) and Maud Olive (29 Jul 1882, WI). In 1878, they settled in Beaver Twp., Clark Co., WI. John was a hardworking man who loved his family. A family story tells of how "Granny Scovel" was terrified of Indians and was nearly scared to death when some of the boys painted their faces and surprised her in the dark of night.

John died at his home 2 May 1910, and is buried in the Greenwood, WI City Cemetery. **Rev. S. E. Sweet** of the Baptist Church conducted the short services, which were held at the Scovel home. In 1925, Mary Ann moved to Ladysmith, WI, to be near her children, John Ezra and Abbie Julia, who had married John Henry Elden Redwine in Neillsville, 9 Sep 1885. Mary Ann died at the home of her son John Ezra, 17 Jun 1926, when she was 83 years old. After a funeral in Ladysmith, she was laid to rest beside her husband.

Farm Named: Pleasant View Farm, owned by John A. T. Scovel, route 3, Greenwood. ." *Greenwood Gleaner, 7 May, 1903*

"Mrs. John Scovel and son Ezra were here Saturday afternoon." *Greenwood Gleaner, 3 Mar 1904*

Frederick J. SHELDON 1839 - 1903 ☆ ⚐
VGR#185 dated 27 Feb 1937

"Fred" was born 16 Oct 1839 in Onondaga Co., NY, the son of Frederick Sheldon (1800, CT), who soon moved the family to Dearborn, MI. He served in the Civil War three years with Co. B, 2nd Mich. Inf. enlisting 10 May 1861 at the age of 21 in Hudson, MI. He was promoted to Full Cpl. 28 May 1861 and to Full Sgt. 27 Sep 1862. He was attached to Co. B, 17th Mich. Inf., 30 Jan 1864, and honorably discharged from Co. B, 2nd Mich. Inf., 6 Jun 1864 at Detroit, MI. He served from the First Bull Run battle to that of the Wilderness and North Anna, including the Spotsylvania Court House, second Bull Run, Fredericksburg, Manassas Junction, Vicksburg, Jackson, Knoxville, and others. During the charge on Knoxville, 96 men were lost in 15 min., and it was there that Fred was wounded in the face. In all, Fred participated in 24 battles. Following the war, he married Ellen E. Clark at Saginaw, MI, 18 Nov 1864. The following July he entered the employ of the USA as a carpenter, and worked at Nashville, TN, for 11 months before returning to Dearborn, MI. During July of 1867, he moved to Fulton, IL, and 10 Dec 1867 he moved to Big Falls on the Popple River, Clark Co., WI. The first winter he worked in the pineries, and in July 1868 he brought his family, including his aged parents, to the area, taking a homestead on the SE 1/4 of the SW 1/4 of sec. 27, Eaton Twp., 1 ½ miles SW of Longwood. "In Greenwood's earliest days, there was no regular dentist, but persons suffering with toothache, if they wished, could go to 'Old Sheldon's' near Longwood and have the tooth removed. He was always found in his bare feet and pulled the tooth with a pair of pliers. This same Sheldon planted many pine trees along the main road near Longwood." *Adapted from The Greenwood History 1853-1934.*

Fred was Justice of the Peace 3 yrs, School Clerk many years, and Town Treasurer 6 years The Sheldons had 6 children: William Adelbert (1866), who lived in Sulphur Springs, MT; Robert L. (Aug 7 1868-Jun 27 1869); Frederick E. (17 Dec 1871-6 Apr 1872); Albertis (1875); Frank L. (1880); and Nancy May (1884). Frederick's sister Mary, the wife of **Peter F. Lantz**, resided near Thorp, WI. Ellen (20 Feb 1848, NY) was the daughter of Brenton Clark of Wheatland, MI. She died 22 Sept 1888. Frederick died 8 Dec 1903 after months of illness. They are both buried in the Greenwood, WI City Cemetery.

"...There are two stones in the [Greenwood] *cemetery with earlier dates, but no one is buried under them. These stones were for two Sheldon children* [Robert L. & Frederick E.] *who died and were buried in the Hackett field (Stoller's). Later the father purchased headstones and wanted to move the bodies of the children but the graves could not be located, so the stones were set up in the cemetery here anyway...." The Greenwood History 1853-1934.*

The actual burial spot is in Warner Twp. sec 2, where the Popple River runs through it. This was later the property of **Wm. H. Mead** (1893), Hans Nelson (1906-1915) and John Stoller (1926).

Plyna H. SHEPARD 1821 – 1889

VGR#534, 20 Jan 1937, Inf. provided by Paul H. Hagedorn, Weston clerk & Herman Schoenherr, Chairman

Plyna Shepard was born 26 Sep 1821 in VT, to Isaac (1776, NH) and Esther (1780, CT). He married Eunice A., who was born 15 Dec 1822 in VT, the daughter of Anni & Elvina Talbot, both natives of NH. Initially Plyna made his living as a shoemaker. Since shoe factories hadn't yet come into existence, this useful trade was a good way for young men to make ready cash. If they were fast, four pairs of soles and heels could be applied in a day to their customers' homemade cowhide shoes, and they'd pocket a dollar before sundown. During 1852 the Shepards left the Green Mountain State and headed west with their three young daughters: Esther (1847), Isadore (1849), and Eunice Emeroy (25 Jul 1851, Royalton, Windsor Co., VT). Ellen E. (Nov 1858) and Charles H. (May 1861) were both born after they were settled in Monroe, Green Co., WI. The couple had 9 children, but only 3 lived into adulthood. At the time of the Civil War, Plyna served as a Pvt. with Co. K, 16th Wis. Inf. having enlisted 12 Dec 1863. He transferred to the US Veteran Reserve Corps, 1 Jul 1864, and was mustered out 29 Jul 1865. During the summer of 1870, the family moved to Clark Co., WI, at a time when there were only 15 dwellings in Neillsville. They witnessed the conversion of the area's vast forests into beautiful farms. They settled in Tioga, but also made two trips to Kansas in a covered wagon with a party of family and friends. The Shepards were farming in Weston Twp. when the 1880 Census was taken. When Plyna died 10 Jan 1889, he was laid to rest in the West Weston Cemetery, Clark Co., WI, in sec. 20, lot #12. In widowhood, Eunice made her home with her son Charles and his wife Dicia in Greenwood. Her daughters, Emeroy (Mrs. Andrew) Loy, and Ellen (Mrs. Lafayette) Bartle, lived nearby. Edna Shepard (13 Oct 1897) was one of ten grandchildren who could put a smile on Eunice's face. That baby had not yet taken her first steps when she was buried next to her grandfather in the West Weston Cemetery, 13 Apr 1898. A new grave was opened next to them 18 Nov 1905, after the family said their last good-byes to Grandma Shepard.

Abram Henry SHOEMAKER 1837 - 1923 ☆

1895 Special WI Veterans Census

Abram was born 27 Oct 1837 in Binghamton, NY, the son of John H. and Jerusha Shoemaker. His parents were both natives of NY. When he was 16 years old, the Shoemakers moved to Summit, Waukesha, WI, where Abram worked as a painter. His siblings were Jacob, Lorenzo, Charles (22 Apr 1849, Gilboa, NY), Margaret, Arlow "Arthur," and Sarah. After eight years he returned to the Empire State where he enlisted with Btry. B, 4th NY H. A., 23 Sep 1861 at Gilboa, NY. His regiment, under the authority of Col.

T. D. Doubleday, was organized in New York City and became known as "Doubleday's Heavy Artillery." They left for Washington 10 Feb 1862, and served near Washington D.C. Their 1st camp was 5 mi. from the Washington, D.C., Chain Bridge over the Potomac.

Upper Battery at Chain Bridge, 1862

Abram received a disability discharge at Ft. Corcoran, VA, 31 Jul 1862 and that fall he married 17 yr. old Elizabeth A. Mattice, 19 Oct 1862. She was born Apr 1845, in Blenheim, NY, where their wedding took place. Her parents were Isaac and Aurilla (Collins/Reynalds) Mattice. The Shoemaker children were all born in WI: Arthur (1865-1946), Charles (Jul 1870-1920 in an explosion), Frank (1872), Anna "Annie" (1874, Mrs. Sharp of Portland, OR), Carl Lincoln (1883-1965), Belva Aurilla (20 Jun 1885-19 Mar 1968, m. Clarence R. Greene of Greenwood, 1905) and Frances (d. age 2 yrs., and is buried in the Greenwood Cemetery). Arthur married Eda Hall and Charles married her sister Lucy. The 1870-1880 census records reported the Shoemakers residence in Otter Creek, Eau Claire Co., WI, and the 1885 Veteran's Census listed their Augusta address. They had purchased 80 acres of land in Eau Claire Co., 10 Apr 1874 and another 40 acres 30 Dec 1874. The next summer, 30 Jul 1875, they purchased an additional 40 acres in Price Co., WI.

Abram & Elizabeth (Mattice) Shoemaker

The Shoemakers also owned property in sec. 16, Thorp Twp. and later resided in Greenwood, WI, (bef. 1905). They eventually resettled in Augusta where they spent the remainder of their lives and are buried. Abram passed away 26 Feb 1923, after an illness of several weeks. He was a faithful soldier for his country, a loyal member of the G.A.R., and his loyalty to the old flag was an inspiration to others. He'd faithfully served his county during some of its darkest hours and gave the same conscientious loyalty to his loved ones and friends.

"A. H. Shoemaker has purchased some of Elias Peterson lots on the east side of town and will build a home as soon as they can get around to it." *Greenwood Gleaner, 18 Apr 1902*

"Mr. and Mrs. Shoemaker from Withee called Sunday at Aug. Noah's." *Greenwood Gleaner, 22 Jul 1909*

Zephaniah SILVERS 1834 - 1911 ☆

VGR 524, dated 6 Feb 1937, Next of kin: Morgan & Frank Silvers (sons) of Soldiers Grove, WI

Zephaniah Silvers

"Zeph" was born 23 Jan 1834 in Mechanicsburg, Champaign, OH, the son of Francis M. and Mary (McIntyre) Silvers, and brother of Teter Myers (1828) and William (1837). His fraternal grandparents were Dr. William and Mary (Myers) Silvers, Sr. Louisa Catherine married Zeph in Randolph Co., IN, 20 Jul 1854. She was born 30 May 1834, the daughter of John and Elizabeth (Loy) Foust. The Silvers and their daughter Mary Elizabeth (13 Apr 1855) moved from IN to Marietta, WI, where 3 more daughters were born: Lucinda J. (12 Jan 1857), Matilda Ann (25 Nov 1859, m. Joseph Adams), and Louisa C. (20 Aug 1862), who was named after her mother. They had returned to IN by the time their son, Francis M. was born, 28 Nov 1864. "Frank" was just 2 months old when Zeph and his brother-in-law Martin V. Foust signed up with Co. A, 147th Ind. Inf., 24 Jan 1865. Thirty year old Pvt. Silvers stood 5'5", had a fair complexion, gray eyes and brown hair. His unit was organized in Indianapolis and mustered in 13 Mar 1865, leaving for Harper's Ferry, WV, 3 days later. They attached to 1st Brigade, 3rd Prov. Div., Army of Shenandoah, did guard duty at Charleston, and participated in the battles of Stevenson's Station and Summit Point, Berryville, Harper's Ferry and Maryland Heights. Pvt. Silvers was honorably discharged with his unit and mustered out 4 Aug 1865. Another brother-in-law, **John T. Foust**, served for Wisconsin during the same period. After Zeph's safe return, the Silvers had 3 sons: David, (14 Oct 1867), Morgan (5 Feb 1871) and Joseph (27 Nov 1873). At the time of the 1880 Census, the Silvers were living in Jefferson, Jay Co., IN, but by 1890, they had returned to Marietta, WI. The family moved to the Greenwood area about 1898 to farm in the Braun Settlement, Warner Twp. Morgan married Betsey Jane Loomis, the daughter of Henry and Margaret Ellen (Foust) Loomis. Joseph married Nora Havens, and when he died 22 Aug 1900 in a logging accident, he was buried in the Greenwood, WI City Cemetery, but has no headstone. Louisa died 11 Aug 1903, and "Grandpa Zeph" passed away 22 Jul 1911, in Morgan's home. Both of them are buried in a shady spot in the Forest Hill Cemetery in Braun Settlement, Warner Twp., Clark Co., WI.

Elezer SISCHO 1825 - 1908 ☆

1885 Special WI Veterans' Census

G.A.R. Memoir of Elezer Sischo, 25 Mar 1825 - 19 Apr 1908

Elezer. Sischo

Elezer "Lee" was born in Washington Co., NY, 25 Mar 1825, the son of Elezer & Debba Sischo. On 21 Sep 1847 he married Mary Ann Prior in Fond du Lac Co., WI. She died 9 Mar 1859, leaving him with 3 children: Betsy Jane (20 Jul 1848), Emma/Emily (2 Aug 1850) and Miles (6 Jul 1852). The 1860 Federal Census (recorded June 1st) listed Lee as a resident of Ashford, WI.

Elezer married a 2nd time 21 Apr 1861 in Fond du Lac Co. His bride was Sarah Ann Baker, born 16 Mar 1842 at Bunker Hill, NY, the daughter of John & Ann Baker, natives of England. Lee and Sarah had two children: Anna "Annie" Jane (5 Apr 1862, m. Clark Isaac Bostwick, 1 Jan 1882) and Manford E. (21 Feb 1864, d. 20 May 1929, Plummer, Benewah Co., ID).

← **Sarah Brown Sischo**

When "Lee" was a resident of Auburn, WI, he enlisted as a Pvt. in the Civil War with Co. G, 14th Wis. Inf. He was mustered in 1 Jan 1862. His records state that he was a 35 year old farmer, stood 5' 6 ½" tall and had black hair, a dark complexion and hazel eyes. He served as a hospital cook. That fall, 3 Oct 1862, he was reported killed during the battle at Corinth, MS, where the Union Army took the victory. Actually, Elezer had been taken captive, and on the 29th was paroled and ordered to St. Louis, MO. He later rejoined his unit and his duties and was mustered out 30 Jan 1865. He served another 10 mos. with US Veteran Vol. Inf., 9th Regt, from Mar 1865 to Jan 1866. At the time of the 1870 Census, Lee was residing in Jacksonport, Door Co., WI, and by 1880 had moved to Kenosha. He and Sarah then moved to Christie, Weston, Clark Co., WI. In 1886, the Sischos moved to MN, and in 1892 Elezer applied for a Civil War Pension while living at Richwood, Becker, MN. He was listed on the Minnesota Territorial Census as a resident of Detroit, MN. He died 19 Apr 1908 in Rockford, WA. Sarah applied for a widow's pension 5 May 1908, in Rockford, Spokane Co., WA. She passed away in Plummer, Benewah Co.,, WA on 25 Jun 1925.

Luther SISCHO 1827 - 1905
1885 Special WI Veterans Census, Christie

Luther was born 18 Apr 1827 in NY. He is believed to have been a brother of **Elezer Sischo**. His family moved from NY to Medina Co., OH, before settling in Wisconsin about 1846. He married Almina "Mina" Brown in Auburn, Fond du Lac Co., WI, 1 Mar 1852. Mina was born 7 Apr 1831 in Sandusky, OH, the daughter of Theodore & Ruth (Collins) Brown. The couple had 8 children: Jesse (10 Apr 1853), Mina (3 Feb 1856), Henry (5 Dec 1859), Frank (25 Mar 1861), Arthur (28 Apr 1867), Edgar (31 Dec 1869), LeRoy Wm. (3 Dec 1873), and Berton (20 Jun 1879). Luther was a resident of Auburn, WI, when he enlisted as a Pvt. in the Civil War with Co. I, 38th Wis. Inf. at age 37. His eyes were hazel, his hair brown, complexion fair and he stood 5' 7" when he volunteered on 31 Aug 1864. He was mustered out 2 Jun 1865 and moved to Osceola, Fond du Lac Co., WI, in 1866. In the spring of 1871 he moved his family to Weston, Clark Co., WI, and is recorded there in 1880, 1885, 1890, 1895 and 1900. In late 1884 Luther filed an application for pension benefits, giving rheumatism as the cause of his disability. He states that his first episode occurred at Petersburg in Jan 1865. This falls within the dates of the Siege of Petersburg (Virginia). A letter in support of his application was submitted by **Albert Tuttle**, another local veteran who served in the same unit. Luther died in Salem, Marion Co., OR on 7 Dec 1905 after a brief illness. When she died 3 Aug 1924 at age 93, Almina was buried next to her husband of 53 years at the City View Cemetery, Salem, OR. She was survived by 30 grandchildren and 15 great-grandchildren. Their granddaughter, Ruth Tilda Sischo, taught in Clark, Jackson, and Marathon Co. schools for 40 years before retiring in 1971.

George W. SLATER, Jr. 1843 - 1904
1885 Special WI Veterans' Census

George was born Aug 1843 in Cayuga Co., NY, the son of **William and Eliza Slater**. On 27 Aug 1861 at Marseilles, IL, he enlisted as Private, joining Co. K, 39th Ill. Inf. in October. He received a disability discharge 25 Sep 1862 after an accidental bayonet wound below his left ear, an injury resulting in deafness, which troubled him throughout his life. On 20 Jan 1864 at Chicago, he enlisted as Private in Co. G / E, 8th Ill. Cav. He mustered out at Benton Barracks, St. Louis, MO, in 1865. Rev. L. E. Eldridge married "George W. Slater of Hayton" and "Malinda E. Alldridge of Brillion" 24 Sep 1868, at Charlestown, Calumet Co.,

WI. Sidney Flansburg and Marian Smith were the subscribing witnesses. Malinda was born 16 Jun 1851 in Bristol, VT, the daughter of Alfred and Malinda E. Alldridge. At the time of the 1880 Census, they were living in Eaton Twp., Clark Co, WI, with their children: George A. (28 May 1869-1951), Warren J. (12 Apr 1872-1921), Alice R. (25 Jun 1874-1943), and Maude Linda/Lulu (13 Jan 1880-1944). George's 63 yr. old father (also a Civil War Veteran) was living with them. Before the new frame school was built in 1881, classes were held in the building adjoining the Slater's residence. Two more children, Frank E. (20 Dec 1888-1957) and William (6 Jul 1892-1936), were born to them before they moved to Laurel, WA. The winter of 1886, George went to Chicago, but did not like it well enough to stay and returned to work in Farling's Lumber Mill. He died 5 Jul 1904 at Fairhaven, WA and was buried 3 days later at Bayview Cemetery, Bellingham, WA, by undertaker W. H. Mock. Malinda died 25 Nov 1919 and was buried beside her husband.

William George SLATER, Sr. 1818 - 1887 ☆ ⚑

VGR#186 dated 25 Mar 1937, Next of Kin: Granddaughter, Mrs. Harry Hogue of Greenwood, WI.

William Slater

The Slater farm in Sec. 27, Eaton Twp., Clark Co., Wisconsin

William was born 2 Mar 1818 in England. He first settled in NY, marrying Eliza (b. 1817) and becoming the father of 3 children, Chantha, George, and Elizabeth, before moving to Spring Prairie, WI, and then to Manlius, IL. On 10 Sep 1861, at Marseilles, La Salle Co., IL, he enlisted with Co. K, 39th Ill. Inf., the same regiment his son George enlisted with a month later. He reenlisted with the Veteran Volunteers at Hilton Head, SC on 1 Jan 1864 and was mustered out at Norfolk, VA, on 6 Dec 1865. After the war he moved to Charlestown, WI, before settling in Clark County. He was crippled with rheumatism, which he attributed to exposure to cold while serving at Deep Bottom, VA. His pension application describes him as 5' 8 ½", 240 lbs, dark complexioned, with gray hair and black eyes. His enlistment papers indicated a height of 5' 10". The Slaters farmed in the SW corner of sec. 27, Eaton Twp. Their neighbors were Jones Tompkins, B. Fentason, Thomas Miller, E. L. Newton, George Huntzicker, John Sythe and **William Fricke**. In 1885 Jones Tompkins, in confirming the validity of William's pension application, told Justice of the Peace James Hewett, "We have been well and personally acquainted for 14 years from 1871 and during that time, William Slater has been afflicted with rheumatism as to entirely disable him and render it impossible to perform manual labor." After Eliza died 8 Jan 1877, William left their farm and moved to Neillsville where his friendly nature was well known. Shortly after receiving an increase in his pension from $10 to $21 a mo., he died 1 May 1887, in the presence of his son George and his daughter, Mrs. Rufnow. His burial was in the Greenwood Cemetery next to his wife.

George Washington SMITH 1833 - 1913
1885 Special WI Veterans Census, Eaton

George was born 25 Nov 1833 in Cato, Cayuga Co., NY, the son of 38 yr. old John Peckham and 39 yr. old Mary Norcross (Patch) Smith. John was a native of Stephentown, Rensselaer Co., NY and Mary was born 3 Feb 1794 in Hamilton, MA. George was a busy married farmer in New Holstein, WI, when the Civil War broke out. At the time of his enlistment with Co. K, 4th Wis. Cav. in Chilton, 24 Feb 1864, he was 30 yrs. old. George and Selana Hammer had married 19 May 1856, in Calumet Co. and he left her with the care of their 6 mo. old son, George Henry (1 Aug 1863, Stockbridge, WI). His son's first two birthdays would pass before their eyes would meet again.

Pvt. Smith had brown eyes, light hair and complexion and stood 6 ft. tall. He received a $60 bounty and a month's advance pay of $13, leaving an outstanding balance of $240 for his 3 yr. term. The next year, during the heat of summer (22 Aug 1865), he was transferred to Co. F. He participated in the campaigns of Baton Rouge and Mobile. The close of the war brought an early end to his obligation and he was mustered out 28 May 1866. His first daughter, Mary Louisa (22 Mar 1867) was born in Gravesville, WI, and the following year Selena died, 3 May 1868. George's second wife was Sarah Addlaide Willets (12 Oct 1853, Beverly, Ontario, Canada). They married in Calumet Co., WI, 2 days before Christmas in 1869. Their children were: Viola L. (2 Dec 1871, Gravesville, m. Coral Young), Sylvester (Aug 1872), Clarissa (5 Jul 1877), Maud (1 Oct 1879), William Henry (27 Oct 1881, Neillsville, m. Angeline L. King), Betsy (7 Jul 1884), Grace (10 Feb 1887), Melissa (23 Mar 1889, Loyal, m. Gus Gustafson), Leon Norman (3 Apr 1891, d. 1918 France-WWI), and

DeForest "Forrest" Franklin (4 Feb 1894, Cleveland, MN, m. Bessie Babb). This family suffered the total destruction of their home in Loyal, WI, 5 Jul 1874. A fire in the kitchen was discovered too late to save anything except a feather and straw bed and sewing machine belonging to G. P. Gwinn, who lived in the main part of the charred house. The home was worth $1,000 but insured for $700. Mr. Gwinn lost all of his possessions, including $200 cash. George's family lost all of their household goods and clothing. The Smiths were in Mayville Twp. for the 1880 Census and 10 May 1882 they were granted a homestead in sec. 6. By 1885 they were living in Eaton and remained there for over 10 years before moving to Kent, Dickey Co., ND, where they lived when the 1910 census was taken. George died in Fullerton, ND, on Independence Day, 1913. Sarah filed for a widow's pension that fall and after nearly 20 years of widowhood, died 28 May 1933 in Sebeka, Wadena Co., MN. They are both buried in Ellendale, Dickey Co., ND.

Thomas J. STEELE 1829 - 1909 ☆
VGR #567, dated 17 Mar 1937, Next of Kin: Art Steele of Greenwood (son)
1885 & 1890 Special WI Veterans Census, Thorp

"Tom" was born in NJ, 3 Jan 1829, the son of William & Mary B. (Shauger) Steele, who moved their family of 12 west to Wisconsin before 1850. He married Jane E., 2 Feb 1853. She was born 11 Jan 1837 in NJ, the daughter of Solomon and Charlotte (Tuttle) Dobbins. During Nov 1863, Tom, then a farm laborer in Plymouth, WI, enlisted as a Pvt. with Co. C, 4th Wis. Cav. Jane was left to care for their children: Charlotte Jane (25 Dec 1854), Mary E. (1856), Catharine (1857), Thomas Jr. (20 Mar 1859), Melissa (1861) and Eliza (1863). Tom was mustered out 22 Aug 1865 as a corporal. Their family grew to include: Hughetta (20 Jul 1867), and Ida Mae (8 Mar 1869). Shortly after Ida's birth, the family settled on a farm in sections 18 & 19, Warner Twp., 4 miles west of Greenwood, WI. Four more children were born there: William R. (1871), Alice Maude (1873), Arthur F. (1874) and Myrtle L. (1878 – d. 1882). The Benjamin School was built in 1871 with the hands of Thos. Steele, Chas. Patterson, **Larry Drinkwine**, Morris & **Curtis Markham** and Mr. Baldwin. Charlotte Jane Steele was hired as the teacher for the first two years Following their retirement, the Steeles moved into the village of Greenwood, residing there for about 20 years. They worshiped at the M. E. Church. Tom was an active member of the G.A.R. and a man of excellent habits and sturdy constitution. He had a cheerful spirit and retained a clear mind up to the last days of his life. Jane died in Greenwood, WI, 29 May 1901, and death took Thomas 26 Oct 1909. Both of them were buried in the East Thorp Village Cemetery, Thorp, WI.

Jack Louis STEVENS 1837 - 1910 ☆
1890 Special WI Veterans' Census, Eaton, Clark Co., WI

Jack was born 10 Oct 1837 in Barton, VT, the 2nd son in a family of 14 children. In 1847, he moved west with his parents, Samuel and Fanny M. Stevens, to settle in Janesville, WI. While residing in IL, he was one of the first responders to Lincoln's call for soldiers at the outbreak of the Civil War, He served with Co. F & E, 9th Ill. Inf. until he was shot through his left thigh during the 2nd battle of Corinth. He then returned to Janesville until his wound healed and he could rejoin. This term lasted until the end of the war and was spent with the 12th Wis. Btry. from 17 Aug 1864 to 7 Jun 1865. After his discharge, Jack went to St. Joe,

MO, joining an overland caravan, and drove 6 mules to Salt Lake City, UT, with a load of merchandise. He encountered many Indians during the trip and a few of his companions were taken. From Salt Lake City, he went on to CA, where he remained until 1888 when he returned to Janesville, WI. The next year, he moved to Greenwood, WI, and made his home with his brother, Perry M. "Peter" Stevens, who was the proprietor of the Commercial House Hotel. The family of **Rudolph Hummel** lived next door to them. For 16 years "Old Jack" was a janitor at the school. In 1906, because of failing health, he was taken to the National Soldiers Home in Milwaukee. He died there Tuesday, 6 Dec 1910, at the round old age of 73 years. Services were conducted by his remaining comrades. His brother Charles took his body to his old home to be buried in Oak Hill Cemetery, Janesville. His surviving siblings were John, Lorinda (Mrs. E. S. Williams), Calista (Mrs. Kelsey), Perry, and Charles.

"Jack" Stevens had his regular annual birthday party at the schoolhouse Monday in which all the children participated to the extent of a large package of candy from the jolly janitor. And Tuesday came the time for "Jack" to express his surprise when the teachers and students presented him with a fine volume and a box of cigars." *Greenwood Gleaner, 3 Nov 1904*

"Jack L. Stevens, who has been the guest of his brother, left for his home in Milwaukee this morning after a most pleasant visit." *Greenwood Gleaner, 26 Aug 1909*

"The expressions that have been gradually gaining a foothold on the faces of several of our bashful bachelors like Chris. Brick, Jack Stevens, George Van Voorhis and a few others, indicate that leap year must have been a disappointment for them. Never mind, it should be remembered that faint heart never won a fair lady." *Greenwood Gleaner, 29 Dec 1904*

National Soldiers Home, Milwaukee, WI

Sylvester Elmer Perry SWEET 1838 – 1917 ☆ ⚑

VGR#188 dated 27 Feb 1937, Next of kin: Wife of Dr. Currie of Greenwood (daughter)

Sylvester E. Sweet

Sylvester was a native of Leeds Co., Ontario, Canada, born 18 Nov 1838, the son of Abijah and Mariah (Rhodes) Sweet. In 1845 his parents moved to Southport, WI and then to Portland, Dodge Co., two years later. In 1854, they went to Bear Creek, Sauk County. Sylvester and his brother Albe enlisted 10 Sep 1861 with the 6th Batry., Wis. L.A. Their brother Nicholas joined the same unit in 1864. Sylvester participated in 9 campaigns, suffering a gunshot wound to the head at Champion Hills, June 1863, and was promoted to Full 2nd Lt. All 3 brothers were honorably discharged 3 July 1865. Sylvester first married Achsa Perry, the daughter of Daniel T. and Salome (Burdick) Perry, at Marble Ridge, WI, 20 Feb 1866. In 1872, after studying at Wayland Academy, Beaver Dam, Sylvester graduated as an ordained minister of the Regular Baptist Church and began preaching at DeSoto, WI. He served as pastor of the Beaver Dam Church two years and supplied the pulpit of the Randolph Church for a considerable time.

Right to left: **Sylvester Elmer Perry Sweet**-father (18 Nov 1838 - 6 Jul 1917); Lewis Elmer Perry Sweet-son (3 Feb 1868 - 1 May 1945); Elmer Wirth Sweet-son (8 Jul 1891 - 22 Feb 1956); John Wirth Sweet-son (29 Dec 1919 - 5 Feb 1921)

His charge of the Trempealeau Church lasted three years and the Monticello Prairie Church two years before he moved to Elkhorn in Nov 1879. The Sweets were the parents of 6 children: Lewis Elmer Perry (3 Feb 1868 -1 May 1945), George E. (1873), Emma E. and Ella E. (1877, twins), Arthur L. (Mar 1885), and Gertrude (24 Sep 1886). Achsa passed away 7 Feb 1903 and was buried at Walnut Hill Cemetery, Baraboo, Sauk Co., WI. While serving the Baptist Church in Greenwood, Sylvester was married to Margaret "Mary" (Foster) Dingley, 19 Jun 1910 by Rev. E. D. Edmunds of Beaver Dam. She was born 29 Oct 1854 at

Hull, Canada, and was the widow of Alfred Dingley who was a stage driver, carpenter and ship builder who died 9 Apr 1906 after freezing both feet in a blizzard on a trip to Beach, ND. Sylvester died 6 July 1917 and Mary passed away 19 Oct 1926. They are buried in the Greenwood, WI City Cemetery.

"Rev. S. E. Sweet left Friday for a several days' visit with his brother, N. L. Sweet at Whitehall, and returned the forepart of the week." *Greenwood Gleaner, 5 Aug 1909*

John E. TATRO 1842 - 1923 ☆

John A. Eaton G.A.R. Post #213 Member, &1890 Veterans' Census, Dist. 143, Walsh Co., ND.

Moses Tatro (father of John)

John was born 23 Jan 1842 in Dunham, Quebec, Canada, and was baptized Jean Baptiste Ducharme, the eldest son of Moyse "Moses" and Marie-Angelique "Mary" (Plante) Tatro. His siblings were: Henriette "Harriet Jane," (ca. 1839, Quebec); Joseph (17 Aug 1843, VT); Thadeus (4 Oct 1845, VT); Zoa (ca. 1848, VT); and Phoebe Ann (8 Feb 1854), Chase (1855) and William (1859)--all 3 born in Madison, WI. At the age of 19, John enlisted 15 Oct 1861 with the Union Army as a Pvt. in Co. E, 4th Minn. Inf. He and his brother Joseph, who was just turning 18, left their Meriden, MN, home to join at Owatonna as some of the first recruits for the Union Army.

Joseph was slightly wounded At the battle at Iuka, MS, 19 Sep 1862, but both boys did return home after the war. During their watch, the victory claimed at Vicksburg led to control of the Mississippi River by Grant's Army from MN to the gulf. John re-enlisted for an additional 3 yrs., 1 Jan 1864 at Huntsville, AL, and was honorably discharged with the rank of Sgt., 7 Aug 1865. Joseph was transferred to the Vet. Reserve Corps, 15 Mar 1865. John married Maria in Owatonna, MN, 3 Mar 1866. She was born 2 Feb 1851, the daughter of Jehiel and Sarah Cass, who owned a neighboring farm. John's brother, Thadeus, married Maria's sister, Olive Cass, 26 Feb 1875. John and Maria were the parents of: Moses Henry (1867), Herbert (1868), Eliza A. (1869), Mary (1871), George Franklin (1874), Pearl Alice (1876), Elsie (1882), and Bertha (Nov 1888, ND). Following Maria's death in 1897, John married Joanna in Crookston, MN, 17 July 1900. She was the daughter of Harold and Sarah (Spencer) Newcomb and was previously the wife of Israel P. Cummings. The Cummings were the parents of 4 children, all born in Whitehall, WI: Olive C. (18 Jun 1872); Asa S. (3 Aug 1874); Sarah J., (16 Jul 1878); and D. Wilbur (21 Aug 1880). In 1902, John served as pallbearer at the funeral of **Hiram Warren Varney** in Greenwood, WI. He also attended the Soldiers Reunion in Neillsville, June 1903, during his residence in Greenwood. By 1920 he was living with his son Moses H. Tatro in Helgeland Twp., MN. John died 1 Apr 1923 at age 80 in Colburn Twp., Chippewa Co., WI, in the home of his son Moses Henry Tatro. His daughter, Elsie (Mrs. George Leslie McElmurry) also resided in Colburn. John's remains were buried beside those of his first wife Maria in the Greenwood Cemetery, at Warren, MN.

Dr. Henry John THOMAS 1850 - 1905
1885 & 1890 Special WI Veterans' Census

Henry was born 26 Jul 1850 in Delhi, Delaware Co., NY, the son of Abram and Olive C. (Lynch) Thomas. The family was living in Ceresco, Fond du Lac Co., WI, when his mother passed away 14 Aug 1853. A year later, in Ceresco, his father married Mary Redfield of Delhi, NY. Two daughters, Florence and Anna, were born to the couple before Abram passed away at age 48 in Ripon, WI. In 1865, at the tender age of fifteen, Henry served with the Union Navy during the Great Civil War. Most young soldiers of his age were drummers and musicians, but this bright recruit was appointed as an apothecary or in civil terms a pharmacist, aboard the USS Dictator.

The "Dictator" was a 4438-ton single-turret seagoing monitor constructed in New York, NY. It was commissioned to serve the Navy in November 1864. However, her power plant problems kept her initial service relatively brief and she was decommissioned that next September 1865 at the League Island Navy Yard, Philadelphia, PA. The Dictator sailed in July 1869 to serve with the North Atlantic Fleet, but was again retired in June 1871. Her final period of commissioned service was spent in the Atlantic coast area between January 1874 and June 1877. Then, in September 1883, the USS Dictator was sold for scrap.

At the close of the Civil War, Henry moved to Chicago and was there when the great fire of 1871 destroyed four square miles of the city. In 1873 he graduated from Rush Medical College.

Dr. Henry J. Thomas
Greenwood, WI's first Doctor.

As a young doctor he moved to Milwaukee, WI, briefly before settling in Greenwood. He was the town's first doctor when he opened his practice on Main St. in a store that was later converted to an implement dealership by Albert and Adolph Schwarze. Like all country physicians, Dr. Thomas rode on horseback or in a buggy through paths in the woods, or over rough corduroy roads to treat his patients who could not make it to town. He was a very successful physician with one peculiarity—he was never seen without a flower in his buttonhole (photo above). Harriett Angelia Andrews, affectionately known as "Gelia," became his bride 3 Oct 1882. She was the daughter of George and Lorinda (Chamberlain) Andrews, born 21 Aug 1859 in Rawdon, Ontario, Canada. Her father was a well-known and respected blacksmith, born near Smith's Falls, Ontario, 3 Dec 1830.

Gelia's parents were some of Greenwood's earliest pioneers. On the 24th of August 1880, a boy named Arthur was born who was raised by Henry and Gelia and always known as their son. This little family resided in Greenwood for approximately eighteen years. Around 1891, they moved to Winston-Salem, NC, where fourteen years later Dr. Thomas had a surprisingly early death at age fifty-five, 29 Nov 1905. It was said he'd never been heard speaking derogatorily about anyone. He was exceedingly popular with the poorer people for many of whom he performed acts of true benevolence. His interment was made in the Masonic plat in the Salem, NC, Cemetery. Afterward, Gelia returned to Greenwood, WI, to live with her sister Mary and brother-in-law Erastus Bowen. She died 22 Jun 1926, at the home of her brother James Andrews after twenty-one years of widowhood. She was buried in Greenwood, WI City Cemetery.

Henry John Thomas

"D. Dangers of Neillsville and Mr. Kessler of Sheboygan leased the property of H. J. Thomas preparatory to putting in a stock of merchandise." *Greenwood Gleaner, 23 Sep 1909--18 yrs ago*

"Dr. H. J. Thomas and wife bid farewell Saturday to their many friends and neighbors leaving on that day for Winslow, N. C., where they went to make their future home." *Greenwood Gleaner, 18 Nov 1909--18 yrs ago*

"A farewell reception was given Dr. H. J. Thomas and wife Friday evening by Mr. and Mrs. John Stewart at the Park House." *Greenwood Gleaner, 25 Nov 1909--18 yrs ago*

Howard Hamilton TOMPKINS 1847 - 1928
Assumed Member of John A. Eaton G.A.R. post #213

Howard was born 17 Oct 1847 in Volney, Oswego Co., NY, son of Alexander Hamilton and Martha (Coe) Tompkins. His siblings were: William H. (1842), Abigail M. (1844), Mary E. (1851), Francis M. (1852), Ruth C. (1856), Edwin M. (1858), Martha E. (1859) and Abraham L. (1860). They were pioneers in the Oswego area, a port town on Lake Ontario in north central NY. Alexander died 23 Feb 1861, when Howard was 13 years old, leaving Martha with a house full of young children, including an infant less than 6 mo. old. Three years later in the depth of winter, Howard said his good-byes to his struggling family and went to Camden, NY, where he enlisted as a Pvt. in Btry. G, 3rd NY L.A.

Howard served from 22 Feb 1864 to 20 Jun 1865 when he was mustered out at Davids' Island, NY Harbor. His company was commanded by Capt. David L. Aberdeen and was active at Wise's Forks and Bennett house. Eliza Melissa Coleman was born in Sussex, England, in 1847, and arrived in Hamilton, NY, with her parents when she was 6 years old. She married Howard 8 Oct 1884 in Chicago, IL, and the couple settled in Warner, Clark Co., WI, where their son Marcus H. was born, 19 Jul 1885. Howard had a property sale during Aug 1889 and traded his farm to L. O. Garrison for the Randall farm ½ mi. north of Greenwood. Howard was granted a 160-acre homestead at the Eau Claire Land Office, 21 Jul 1890, for sec. 22, Butler Twp. This occurred in the midst of a serious depression and a collapse of the American economy which hit farm states like Wisconsin the hardest. This, coupled with a period of unusually harsh weather and a whopping 72" snowfall for the season, made the Tompkins' first year on their homestead stressful. The next winter their biggest problem wasn't money or weather, it was the dreaded epidemic of typhoid fever that was sweeping the county, claiming victims. Eliza contracted it and after her condition was complicated by pneumonia, she died 29 Jan 1892 and was buried in the East Thorp Village Cemetery. On 26 Jun 1900, Howard married his brother's widow, Vianna (Sep 1860, IN), a mother of 5, in Thorp. The family moved to Shaw, OR, where their daughter Laura was born (1903). Howard worked as a U.S. Mail Carrier in the Shaw and Aumsville areas for many years. He passed away 16 Mar 1928 in Klamath Falls, OR, and was buried in Linkville Cemetery. Howard's only daughter, Laura, died in 1931, Vancouver, WA. His son Marcus worked as a mail carrier in FL until his retirement, and passed away 13 Feb 1962 in Tampa.

Albert W. TUTTLE 1830 - 1888
1885 Special WI Veterans Census

Albert, the youngest son of Rensselear (18 Aug 1789, CT) and Clarissa (Crozier, b. 23 Jul 1797, MA) Tuttle, was born 12 May 1830 in the Catskill Mts. of NY. He was married to Caroline L. Ransom in Granville, Licking Co., OH, 30 Dec 1854 by Pastor Irving. Charlotte M. Raymond (the wife of veteran **Calvin J. Mills**) was one of their bridesmaids and was later present at the births of some of the Tuttle children. When he was 33 years old, Albert enlisted in the Civil War under Capt. Phillips at Fond du Lac, WI, 31 Aug 1864. He stood 6 ft. tall, with grey eyes, light hair and a fair complexion. He was a Pvt., trained as a surveyor, and a member of Co. I, 38th Wis. Inf. He served alongside **Luther Sischo**, who eventually became his neighbor. They mustered out at Tennallytown, near Washington D.C., 2 Jun 1865.* He suffered with his service wounds the remainder of his life. In Jan 1867, the Tuttles moved from Fond du Lac to Brown Co. and in Jan 1871 moved to Weston, Twp., Clark Co., WI. Albert's elderly parents accompanied them. Albert and Caroline were the parents of: Elma/Alma (ca.1856), Francelia (20 Mar 1859), Harriet (ca. 1861), Ada/Ida (ca. 1863), Clinton J. (Apr 1870), Cora Ellen (30 Oct 1872), Lillian Maud (24 Aug 1874), and Leva May (25 Nov 1876). They lived on the banks of the Black River in sec. 16, Weston Twp., just across the road from **Calvin Mills** and **Luther Raymond**. Albert's aged parents, "Rancy" and "Clarisy" lived with them, as was typical in the days before Social Security. In this close-knit community, many neighbors were also relatives and Civil War veterans were numerous. Together these brave friends fashioned a civilized society and cleared productive farms in those wild woodlands. Besides farming, Albert surveyed and constructed some area roads, helped plot the East Weston Cemetery (now Chapel Hill), worked on the construction of the Christie Schoolhouse and helped build their M. E. Church.

* (see page 120)

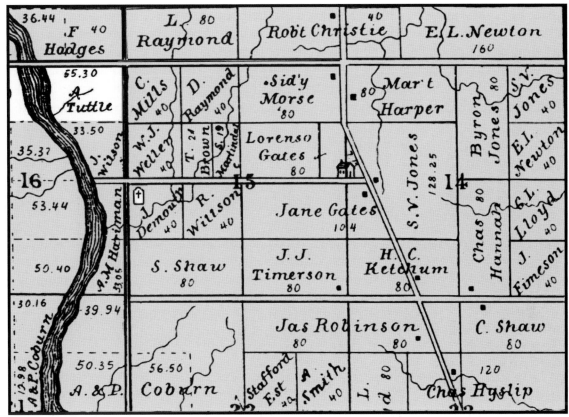

The Heart of Weston Twp., ca. 1882

The Tuttle farm was in section 16. The East Weston Cemetery is southeast of his property, at the Northwest edge of **Jacob Demouth**'s land in section 15.

Everyone seemed to know the Tuttles and when their home and everything in it, including their precious family photos, burned in the spring of 1885, the "boys" helped him erect a new one. It was a cold winter day and a difficult time to dig a grave when Albert died, 13 Dec 1888, at the age of 58. He himself had stood over the open graves of loved ones who were buried there. Caroline was left to raise their youngest children alone. She moved west to live with Leva May's family. After Ada's second marriage to Wm. Edward Wilson following the early death of her first husband, Benjamin Hyslip, Caroline made her home with them. She died 16 Mar 1911 in Woodburn, Marion Co., Oregon.

Hiram Warren VARNEY 1836 - 1902 ☆ ⚑
VGR#189 dated 27 Feb 1937, Next of kin: Charles Varney of Greenwood (son)

Hiram was born 23 June 1836 in Skowhegan, Somerset, ME, the son of Levi and Harriet (Stewart) Varney. He married Cynthia Edith Withee (left) on 13 July 1861 and on their first anniversary enlisted as a Pvt. with Co. A, 19th ME Inf., 13 July 1862. He was honorably discharged 3 June 1865. During his service he lost one of his fingers and had a foot badly crushed. That August, after his discharge from the army, he and his wife moved to La Crosse where they lived for 3 years. A similar span of time was spent in Iowa before they returned to La Crosse for another year and a half. From there they moved to Clark Co., settling in Warner Twp. In August of 1902 they moved off their farm and were living in Harry Hogue's house while building a cozy home of their own across the street. They were just a few weeks away from settling in their own new home, where plastering was underway, when their plans changed abruptly. That Saturday morning, 25 Oct 1902, Hiram had an attack of chronic diarrhea, an affliction he suffered with many times following his days in the army. The next morning he built the fire and did the chores. About 9 o'clock, however, he felt chilled and sat by the fire to warm himself. Finally determining he had an attack of grip coming on, he decided to walk up to Dr. Schofield's office.

Cynthia talked him into letting her go instead and returned with some medicine that she gave to him at 10:45. A half-hour later she administered a second dose. After resting on the lounge, Hiram had a fainting spell and asked that the doctor be called, but before he was summoned, he showed signs of the fast approaching crisis. Within a few minutes, without any apparent suffering, death had claimed its own. His body was laid to rest in the Greenwood, WI City Cemetery. The G.A.R. attended the funeral in a body.

Cynthia Varney

The pall bearers were: **John Booth, Charles Cummings**, **John W. Stanton**, **William Oelig**, **Paschal Wallis,** and **John Tatro**. Cynthia passed away 25 Oct 1915 and was buried at Hiram's side. The family worshiped at the Grace M. E. Church. The Varneys were the parents of: Charles Abraham Lincoln (25 Apr 1865, Skowhegan, ME, m. Nettie May VanAirsdale); Perley Forrest (19 Jun 1867* d. 4 Aug 1868, La Crosse); Alba Forrest (2 Dec 1869, Carpenter, IA m. Belle C. VanAirsdale); Edith Ellora (27 Jan 1872*, was a music teacher at Medford, d. Denver, Co. 5 Apr. 1950, buried in Greenwood); Louisa "Lulu" Alice (6 Apr 1875* m. Henry Warner); Ralph Lester (30 Jan 1877** m. Henrietta Gertrude Bartlett); Mabelle Florence (6 Jan 1882** m. Ronald M. Lamont); and Maud Beatrice (21 Nov 1884** m. Chester D. Huffmire). *Born in La Crosse, WI, **Born in Greenwood, WI

"Mrs. Cynthia Varney sold her cattle and sheep from the farm to John Shanks. A. F. Varney and Denver Green drove them to Greenwood Thursday." *Greenwood Gleaner, 2 Jul 1903*

Dallas M. VERNAM 1844 – 1908
1885 Special WI Veterans Census, Neillsville

Dallas was born August 4, 1844, the son of John & Clarissa (Beswick) Vernam. He was the youngest of their 7 children and his siblings were: Miles, Sally Ann, Marcus, George, Roxy Ann and John Henry. His half-sister, Esther Ann, was five years younger. He was married to Mary Jane Roberts 3 Jul 1866 at Warrensburg, NY. He resided in Bolton for six years, when he moved his family west, settling in Clark Co., WI, in 1872. They had two daughters: Clarissa, who was named for Dallas' mother and died 31 Jan 1869 at 11 mo., and Carrie Bell

(Mrs. Wilder L. Newell). Dallas was a Civil War Veteran who enlisted in Co. H, 93rd NY Inf. Regt. as a Pvt. on 10 Nov 1861 for 3 years, and was discharged 12 Dec 1862 at Philadelphia by reason of Surgeon's Certificate for disability. He re-enlisted in Co. E., 142nd NY Inf., 1 Sep 1864 to serve a year, and was discharged 7 Jun 1865 at Raleigh, NC. In 1880, the Vernam family resided in Christie, sec. 11 of Weston Twp., his closest neighbors being Robert Christie and E. L. Newton. He later moved to Neillsville, where they lived for 25 years. Dallas died 12 Jan 1908 at his home in Neillsville, at the age of 64 after suffering greatly for quite some time. Rev. W. P. Burrows conducted the funeral in the home. Dallas was a brother and neighbor of Roxy Ann (Thomas) Chadwick and a half-brother to Esther Ann (Hiram) Jebo of Tuppers Lake, NY. Mary Jane passed away 11 Jul 1931 at the age of 81. Both Dallas and Jane are buried in the Neillsville, WI City Cemetery.

Thomas R. VINE 1846 – 1920 ☆

"Tom" was born 17 Jun 1846 in Buffalo, NY, to Thomas and Mary Vine. His brothers were: John Thomas, Benjamin and Frank. He moved to Lynn Twp., Clark Co., WI in 1862, where he enlisted as a Pvt. with Co. I, 14th Wis. Inf., 30 Dec 1863. During 2 yrs. of service, he participated in the battles of Shiloh, Vicksburg, Nashville, Tupelo, the skirmish on White River, the march from Brownsville to Pilot Knob, the campaign against Montgomery, the Missouri campaign, Lookout Mountain, Red River, Spanish Fort, Ft. Blakely, Ft. De Russa, and many others. He was mustered out 9 Oct 1865 at Mobile, AL.

Emma E., a daughter of Matthew Marvin, married Tom 19 Oct 1868. She was born 26 Apr 1852 in NY and later moved with her parents to Greenwood, WI. The Vines were the parents of: Edward C., Ernest R., Alice E. who married Bert Monroe, Jeremiah "Jerry" T., and Percy L. The family lived in sec. 25, Warner Twp. on what later became the farm of Leonard Johnson about 2½ mi. NE of Greenwood. In later life, they moved into Greenwood where Tom was an active member of the G.A.R. and the I.O.O.F. In 1910 the Vines took a homestead claim in Vida, MT. After proving up their land they, along with their son Ernest, moved to Elk River, ID. The ledger of the Central Hotel confirms a return visit Thomas made to Greenwood 17 Jun 1917 from his home in Poplar, MT. Thomas died there 24 Nov 1920 and was buried in St. Marie's Cemetery, Benewah Co., ID. "Grandma Emma" passed away at the ripe old age of 92 years, 10 Oct 1944, and was laid to rest in Moscow, ID.

"Mrs. Thos. R. Vine, who with her husband recently returned from a visit with relatives at Rice Lake and other points, brought us in a sample of Indian rice which was gathered while away. It is used by many for food and is pronounced a good dish." *Greenwood Gleaner, 6 Oct 1904*

Paschel Brooks WALLIS 1840 - 1922 ☆ 🏳

VGR#191 dated 27 Feb 1937, Next of Kin: Dean Wallis (Son)

Paschel was born 24 August 1840 in Jefferson Co., NH. He moved to Wisconsin as a child, settling in Grant Co. He enlisted with Co. K, 47th Wis. Inf., 23 Jan 1865 serving as a Pvt. and was discharged 11 Sept 1865. On 12 Mar 1867 he was married to Orzina Dean (25 Oct 1842, NH), the daughter of Elhanan Winchester and Louise Dean. Orzina's first husband, Joshua Davis, and her father were both members of Co. C, 2nd Wis. Cav. and neither lived to return to civilian life. Her father fell first in Missouri in 1863 and Joshua died in Tennessee in 1865. In 1885 the Wallis family moved to Clark Co., WI where for many years, Paschel drove the stage from Neillsville to Withee. As they aged they moved into Greenwood where Orzina had a carpet weaving business. Their oldest son, Dean, lived next door.

The Wallis children were: Dean Wilton (14 Jul 1874, Bloomington, WI, m. Alice Langley, d. 2 Jul 1947 in Clayton, WI); Idella Grace (Feb 1878, m. Walter Millard); Blanche M. (Jun 1884, m. Barton Marvin); and Vern A. (adopted Jun 1890). When Orzina was gravely ill, her sister, Mrs. Horace Atwood of Bridgeport, WI, visited her. After Orzina died 12 Jul 1906, Paschel married Mrs. Laura Redfield 17 Sep 1907. A big attraction was scheduled during the county fair, Friday at 2 pm, for 72 year old Paschel to announce his intention of being married at the fairgrounds to Mrs. Redfield who was 78 years young. A $35 bedroom suite was given to the newlyweds as a wedding gift. Laura died 8 Feb 1914 and Paschel died on 17 January 1922 and was laid to rest with military honors in the Greenwood, WI City Cemetery, next to Orzina.

"P. Wallis broke down with his stage near Tom Chadwick's, and the latter's wagon had to be mustered into Uncle Sam's service to get the mail to its destination. *Greenwood Gleaner, 2 Dec 1909--10 yrs ago*

"Mrs. P. Wallis slipped and fell on Saturday, spraining her left limb so badly that it layed her up almost all winter." *Greenwood Gleaner, 16 Dec 1909--15 yrs ago*

"Stage driver, Paschal Wallis purchased a dandy new wagon for his mail and stage route." *Greenwood Gleaner, 26 Aug 1909--10 yrs ago*

Henry C. WELSCH 1840 - 1912 ☆ 🏳

VGR#192 dated 27 Feb 1937, Nex of kin: Mrs. A. L. Armstrong of Greenwood (niece)

Henry Welsh

Henry was born in Prussia 2 March 1840, having immigrated to the USA in 1847 with his parents, Daniel & Mary Catherine, who farmed in Sheboygan Co., WI. At the age of 22 years, Henry enlisted with Co. H, 26th Wis. Inf., 18 Aug 1862. Pvt. Welsch (aka Welsh) was 5' 8" tall, had blue eyes, light brown hair and a fair complexion. After surviving a gunshot wound to the right temple during the Battle of Chancellorsville 2 May 1863, he was given an honorable disability discharge 14 Oct 1863 and not considered fit for reenlistment. Emma Seidel (1843-1886) became his wife 12 Nov 1863. Their ten children were: Daniel P. of Spokane, WA; Anna (Mrs. Halbert A.) Bright of Bright; Minnie (Mrs. Thos. J.) Selves of Colby; Henry Jr. of Colby; William F. of Spokane, WA; Louise "Lulu" (Mrs. Julius) Palmetier of Los Angeles, CA; Emma (Mrs. Daniel Conway, Mrs. Frank G.) Pope of Colby; Paulina "Lena" (Mrs. Bert S.) Barber of Minneapolis, MN; Louis of N. Chicago, IL; and Richard, who died at age 1. They purchased land in sec. 24, Town of Colby (now Green Grove Twp.) during 1876, and resided there except for a short time spent in Hemlock in the mercantile business. In 1887, soon after the death of his wife, the family moved to Colby, WI. In May 1890 he was married to Mrs. Emma (Thistle) Penny, from whom he was later divorced (Mar 1899). On 7 Dec 1909, he was united in marriage to Sophia L. (Johnson) Rossman of Marshfield. Henry was a member of the I.O.O.F. and the G.A.R. The morning of 21 Feb 1912, Henry was up and about town as usual and returned home near the supper hour, but did not appear for dinner the next day at the home of his daughter, Mrs. Tom Selves. His son-in-law went to his house and found Henry lying fully dressed, dead in his bed, just ten days short of age 72. He was buried in the Greenwood, WI City Cemetery where he was laid to rest at the side of his wife and child.

William H. WHEELER 1834 - 1910
VGR#531, Next of kin: Asa Duell of Greenwood (son-in-law) & Informant, Claude Mills

William was born 28 Apr 1834 in VT, and raised in Ft. Edward, NY, the son of Samuel and Jane (Finton) Wheeler. Both parents were natives of VT and Samuel was a farmer and carpenter. William served in the Civil War before moving to Clark Co., WI, about 1888. Even though he was only a resident of Christie, WI, for around five years, he was respected and esteemed for being a home loving, God fearing, family man. He married Lucinda, the daughter of Benjamin and Jane Van Buren, in 1860. She was born during July 1844 at Ticonderoga, NY on the "Old Fort Ground". The Wheeler children were: Ida L. (13 May 1863, m. Asa A. Duell of Greenwood), Cora E. Lamb of Ft. Edward, NY, Wm. "Frank" of Christie and Carl H. of Warrensburg, NY. William passed away at 4 p.m., Monday, 25 Apr 1910 of heart failure; just three days shy of his 76th birthday. His funeral was held at the Christie Church and his remains were buried in the Chapel Hill Cemetery. Lucinda died 22 Oct 1918 of Spanish Influenza in Thorp, WI, at the home of her son, Frank, and was buried beside her husband.

"Wm. Wheeler had a cow break its leg last week." *Greenwood Gleaner, 10 Mar 1904*

"Mrs. Wm. Wheeler visited at her daughter's Mrs. Asa Duel the later part of last week." *Greenwood Gleaner, 3 Nov 1904*

Isaac WILCOX 1847 - 1922
1885 Special WI Veterans' Census

Isaac was born in Warrensburg, Warren Co., NY, 8 Mar 1847. Enlisting in the Civil War at age 18 with the Union Army, Co. D, 16th NY H. A., he served his country until 21 Aug 1865. After the war, he moved to Clark Co., WI, where he married Clara M. Wilson, 20 Nov 1875.

For 28 years they resided on their farm in sec. 23 of Weston Twp., near Christie. Four children were born to them: Maude Redmond of Portland, OR, Blanche Churchill Talbott, Ralph of Killdeer, ND, and Marion Post of Billings, MT. About 1904, Isaac and Clara moved to Portland, OR, residing there until 1911 when they moved to Quinion, Billings Co., ND, to homestead. Six years later, Isaac suffered a stroke of paralysis. His health steadily declined until a third stroke rendered him entirely helpless, and he passed away the morning of 7 Jun 1922. His casket was covered with the flag, a military salute was fired over the grave, and taps sounded as his remains were laid to rest right on the homestead in Quinion. For him, last taps were sounded as he answered the last roll-call at the age of 75 yrs., 2 mos. and 29 days.

Lewis Henry WILCOX 1842 - 1907 ☆

Lewis Henry was born in Ripley Twp., Chautauqua Co., NY, 14 Nov 1842, the son of Charles Winthrop and Emily (Palmer) Wilcox. He came with his parents to Dodge Co., WI, in 1853 and then to Waupaca Co. the following year. Two of his siblings, Winthrop and Charles Adelbert Wilcox, later lived at Weyauwega, as did their mother. His brother, Sheldon Edgar Wilcox (b.1850, married Sarah Ann Baker), lived in IA and his sister, Mary (Vernon) Mumbrue (1845), lived in Lind, WI. In 1861 Lewis enlisted as a Private in Co. A, 8th Wis. Inf. and served through the war, mustering out 5 Sep 1865 at Demopolis, AL. He joined the John A. Eaton G.A.R. Post in 1902. In Oct 1867 he married Anna Louise, daughter of John and Mary (Cobb) Hayward, at Royalton, Waupaca Co., and became the father of 4 children: Walker and Pearl (James) Murphy, both of Fifield, Orpha (Thomas) Billings, who died at Fifield, 25 Jan 1901, and Lewis E., who moved west. Lewis and Anna located in Park Falls, WI in 1872 or 1873 and remained there a number of years. They moved to Greenwood, WI, in 1894, where Lewis worked for the N. C. Foster Lumber Co. until the close of that lumbering business. He was well known by the local woodsmen and had many friends among them. He lived on a farm NE of town and when in the village, he usually made his home with Harry Hogue and family. Louis died 24 Dec 1907 and was buried at Fifield next to his daughter, Orpha.

Reuben WILSON 1822 - 1902 & George M. WILSON 1843 - 1919
1885 Special WI Veterans Census, Christie & Neillsville

Reuben was born 4 March 1822 in Jefferson Co., NY. In 1841, he married Lucy, born 22 Jun 1824 in Ellisburg, NY. During the Civil War he served as a Fifer/Musician with Co. K, 24th NY Inf. He enlisted 7 May 1861 at the age of 39 and, as Full Fife Major, received a disability discharge 30 Apr 1862 at Alexandria, VA. His son, George M. Wilson (May 1843, NY), enlisted 9 Sep 1862, serving as Bugler with Co. H, 3rd Wis. Cav., and then with the U.S. Veteran Reserve Corps, receiving his discharge 19 Dec 1864. In Dec 1867, George married Eliza Jane Russell (1849, NY), and their children, Reuben's grandchildren, were: Marion (Mrs. Wm. Telfer; Oct 1868-Jul 1910) and Frank (May 1881). Reuben and Lucy's daughter, Sarah Jane (Aug 1854, NY), married Henry James Jones in Jefferson Co., WI, in 1871. The couple had 6 children. Both Reuben and George resided in Weston Twp., Clark

Co., WI, when the 1880 Census was recorded. Reuben's wife Lucy passed away 20 Jun 1893. Reuben died 27 Apr 1902 in Duluth and his funeral was held at the Christie Church. Both burials were made in what is today called "Chapel Hill Cemetery", formerly known as "Weston East Cemetery". George's family moved west and George died in Scotts Mills, Marion Co., OR, 29 Jul 1919. Eliza filed for her widow's pension there. Sarah Jane passed away at the home of her daughter, 9 Nov 1933, in Sparta, WI.

Andrew WING 1832 – 1915 ☆
1885 Special WI Veterans Census

Andrew was born in Oswego, NY, 4 Dec 1832, the son of Joseph Kellsey and Lydia (Brown) Wing. In adulthood, he located in New Chester, Adams Co., WI, where he married Amanda/Almeda A. Hartson, 5 Nov 1856. She was born 22 Apr 1840 in Kishwaukee, IL. The Wings had 6 children: Martin Luther Wing of Neillsville (m. Nellie Scott); Mrs. Clara Winchester, who passed away 15 Sep 1909; Emily (George) Bell of Oxford; Mrs. Chas. Page of Endeavor; Ida E. (James Thomas) Wedding of Neillsville who was born 3 Apr 1870; and Estella A. (Henry) Nelson of Oxford, WI. Andrew served in the Civil War with both Co. G. 19th and Co. D 38th Wis. Inf. He enlisted 11 Feb 1862, was discharged for a disability and re-enlisted 31 Mar 1864, then was transferred out 24 Apr 1865. After his wife died 28 Mar 1878, he moved to Clark County in the spring of 1879 and resided in Weston Twp. until the fall of 1903. Later he married Mary Jane, the daughter of John and Eva Flint. She was born in Onondaga, NY, 19 Jul 1840 and moved with them to Wisconsin as a small child. She first married George Henry Forbush at Beaver Dam, WI, 28 May 1859. She and George had 6 sons and 2 daughters. Her second marriage to Andrew Wing took place 5 Jul 1878. One daughter, Laura (Cora Irene) Moffat of Hewettville, was born to them Oct 1866 in Spring Bluff, WI. In their senior years, Andrew and Mary lived in Neillsville. When his health declined, he moved to Maston Hall at the Veterans' Home, 13 Oct 1903. The next month Mary was also admitted, 3 Nov 1903. Andrew's comrades thought well of him. He passed away on the morning of 28 Dec 1915 in the hospital at the Veterans' Home and was buried in the Veterans Memorial Cemetery, King, Waupaca, WI, sec. 3, Lot 19, Grave 19. Mary Jane died 27 May 1916 and was buried in the Neillsville, WI, City Cemetery.

Christian WOLLENBERG 1843 - 1916 ☆ 📖
VGR#193 dated 25 Ma 1937, Next of kin: H. J. Wollenberg of Alexandrine Av., Detroit, MI (son)

Christopher J Wollenberg

"Chris" was born in Brandenburg, Germany, 17 Mar 1843, the son of Christian and Mary (Hass) Wollenberg. The family immigrated to New York State in 1844 and settled on a farm. Chris bought 40 acres of his own in Orleans Co., NY where he farmed for three years before moving to Rochester, NY to learn the butcher's trade, which he followed for four years. At Lockport, NY, Chris enlisted with the Union Army, Co. A, 129th NY Inf. and was honorably discharged 28 Dec 1862. He then enlisted with Co. L, 5th US Arty, 29 Dec 1862, and served until 22 Aug 1865.

He was in 18 engagements, including battles at Fisher's Hill, Mt. Jackson, Port Republic, and Winchester, VA, where he was taken prisoner. He was held at Richmond from 15 Jun 1863 until receiving parole at City Pt., 19 Jul 1863. He also participated in the battle of Cedar Creek, where Sheridan recovered the victory by his famous ride. Chris' service ended 22 Aug 1865 at Camp Bailey, MD. His next two years were spent in Wolcottville, NY before he moved to Valley Creek, MN, to buy and sell cattle. Albertine married Chris 25 Oct 1866. She was born 4 Jun 1843, the daughter of Martin Wendt. Her family had first settled in NY in 1862, then 5 years later moved to Woodbury, MN. The Wollenberg children were: Charles (16 Jul 1867); Gustav (11 May 1871); Edward F. (26 Sep 1873); Henry (22 Jan 1876); Emma (20 Nov 1877, m. John Syth); Ferdinand (6 Mar 1880, the Greenwood State Bank cashier); Rosa (20 Apr 1881); and Ella (28 Jun 1886, m. Dr. Karl Baker). Besides the G.A.R., Chris belonged to the Odd Fellows Lodge. Albertine died 22 May 1904 and was buried in the Greenwood, WI City Cemetery.

When Chris passed away 27 Sept 1916, he was laid to rest beside her. In 1884, Wollenberg's Market opened in Greenwood, WI. A new brick building was built 15 years later. At the turn of the century, another market was opened in Spencer and operated for 3 years before the family resumed their business in Greenwood, selling out when Chris retired in 1909. The market was then converted to the Central Hotel.

Wollenberg Meat Market, Greenwood, WI
*Chris is in the white apron

"The carpenter work on the Wollenberg building was started under the direction of S. H. Butcher and B. L. Bailey." *Greenwood Gleaner, 5 Aug 1909--10 yrs ago*

Lucien "Vernon" ZANDER, Jr. 1847 - 1931 ☆

1885 Special WI Veterans' Census

Lucian V Zander Jr

"Vernon" was born 28 Nov 1847 at 4th St., Troy, NY, the son of Lucien Vernon and Rebecca Anna (Whitney) Zander. At age 16, while residing in Jefferson, WI, Vernon enlisted with Co. B, 3rd Wis. Inf., 21 Aug 1864 as a substitute for Charles Stoppenbach of Jefferson. He was 17 years old, 5' 2½" tall and had a fair complexion, light brown hair and hazel eyes. He participated in the battles of Averysborough and Bentonville, where he was wounded, and the Grand Review* in Washington D.C. He was mustered out 9 Jun 1865. By May 1875, he was living in Cold Springs, WI, and 28 Nov 1877 married 24 yr. old Alice Josephine in Whitewater, WI. She was the daughter of Dr. Seth Griswold and Mary B. Pickett, born 1 Jul 1853 in Ashford, WI. The Zander's first daughter, Ethel Mae, was born in Hebron, WI, 21 Nov 1879. Shortly after her birth, they moved to Christie, Sec. 4, Weston Twp., WI, where their next 3 children were born: Glenn Vernon (25 Oct 1884), Milton Ward (10 Nov 1886), and Merle Amelia (13 Sep 1889). Irma Florence (21 Jan 1897) and Adela Carrie (17 Sep 1899) were born in Elgin, IL. From 1900-1903, the Zanders lived in Crowley, LA. Their last residence was 15½ 26 Ave., Venice, CA. Vernon applied for a military pension 17 Jul 1890 and his wife applied for a widow's pension 18 Sep 1931. Vernon died 5 Aug 1931 at the **Sawtelle Veterans Home**, Los Angeles, CA, and was buried in Pomona, CA. Alice passed away 4 Jun 1933 in Pomona.

As one of his last official acts, Abraham Lincoln created the Old Soldiers' Homes, to house disabled veterans of the Civil War.

← **The Sawtelle Home** (1888) was the first one to open west of the Rockies.

* (see page 120)

CEMETERIES

The Q.M.'s Department provided for interments of soldiers who died in battle. Burial grounds were first opened near general hospitals and cemeteries were later established in the combat zones as memorials to Union soldiers who gave their lives in battle. Preserving records of deceased soldiers and of their places of burial was a problem faced by the War Department early in the conflict.

War Department General Order No. 55, 11 Sept 1861, delegated to Commanding Officers the responsibility for the burial of military personnel who died within their jurisdictions. It also directed them to preserve accurate and permanent records of deceased soldiers and their place of burial. The Q.M. General was ordered to place a registered headboard at the head of each soldier's grave. It immediately became obvious that the new burial policy carried no provisions for acquiring burial lands. Attempts were made to acquire soldiers' plots in cemeteries near large general hospitals, where many soldiers had passed away. It contained some 15,000 burials. The program was pushed with equal vigor in the Military Division of TN. The program rapidly approached the point of peak performance. In all areas of the continental theater, 87,664 remains had been re-interred in 41 national cemeteries. The total number of interments by June 30, 1866 was 104,528.

Establishment of National Cemeteries

Pursuant to the Act of July 17, 1862, fourteen national cemeteries were created in the latter half of that year. One cemetery was established at **Alexandria, Virginia**. The City of Alexandria was the site of one of the principal concentration camps for northern troops sent to defend Washington at the outbreak of hostilities between the North and South. The cemetery at the **Soldiers' Home** was made a national cemetery for purposes of administration.

The figures portray the historically verified encounter between Confederate Brigadier Gen. Lewis Addison Armistead and Capt. Henry Harrison Bingham who was an aide to **Union Major General Winfield Scott Hancock** on Cemetery Ridge during Picket's charge of July 3 1863. This attack became known as the "High Tide of the Confederacy" Although Armistead and Hancock had been long time friends and fellow officers, their political differences came between them at the outbreak of the Civil War.

Armistead joined the newly formed Confederacy while Hancock chose to stay by the flag of the United States. Both officers served their counties well and were promoted into leadership positions. After the two men went their separate ways, it was twenty-seven months before they were to meet again. This meeting finally took place on the battlefield remembered forever as "Gettysburg." During Pickett's charge, both officers were wounded. Armistead was mortally wounded and Hancock received a wound from which he would be in hospital care for many months. Armistead's cries for help were heard by several officers nearby, and it was a fellow fraternity brother, Captain Bingham, who arrived and offered aid to his fallen comrade-in-arms. Armistead spoke of his close relationship with Hancock and he asked Captain Bingham to relay a message to his friend. He entrusted his personal effects to the captain. Armistead died two days later at the George Spanger farm hospital site. *Gettysburg National Cemetery*

This marble sarcophagus at **Cold Harbor** National Cemetery contains 889 unknown dead from burial trenches at Cold Harbor, Savage Station, Gaines Mill, and Mechanicsville Battlefields around Richmond, Virginia. It is only 5 feet high and was built in 1877 by the US Government.

Two old post cemeteries, **Fort Leavenworth** and **Fort Scott**, both in Kansas, were incorporated into the system. Seven national cemeteries were established at troop concentration points, including **Philadelphia**, Pennsylvania; **New Albany,** Indiana; **Danville**, Kentucky; **Camp Butler**, Illinois; **Keokuk**, Iowa; **Loudon Park**, Maryland; and **Annapolis**, Maryland. One was opened at **Cypress Hills**, New York, for burial of the remains of Confederate prisoners and guards who perished in a train wreck.

A unique feature of this program was the decision to transform the burial sites on battlefields of the war into national cemeteries. One was established near **Sharpsburg**, Maryland, as a memorial to the dead who fell in the Battle of Antietam. Another was located on the battlefield at **Mill Springs**, Kentucky.

As the civil conflict continued to rage, the number of national cemeteries continued to increase. Six cemeteries were created in 1863, including **Gettysburg**, Pennsylvania, which is now maintained by the Department of the Interior; **Beaufort**, South Carolina; **Cave Hill** in Louisville, Kentucky; **Knoxville**, Tennessee; **Lexington**, Kentucky; and **Rock Island**, Illinois. In 1864, national cemeteries were established at **Beverly**, New Jersey, and **Mound City**, Illinois. Also established that year was the **Battleground** National Cemetery in Washington, D.C., which is operated and maintained by the Department of the Interior, and **Arlington** National Cemetery, which is operated by the Department of the Army.

Following the close of the Civil War in 1865, there was increased activity in the development of existing national cemeteries and the need to establish new burial grounds. National cemeteries were established that year at **Balls Bluff**, VA; **Florence**, SC; **Mobile**, AL; **Raleigh**, NC; and **Salisbury**, NC. The **Stones River** National Cemetery in Murfreesboro, TN, **Andersonville** National Cemetery in Andersonville, GA; and the **Fredericksburg** National Cemetery in Fredericksburg, VA, all of which are operated and maintained by the Department of the Interior, were also established that year. The Secretary of War directed the purchase of additional land for cemetery use. In 1867, 17 national cemeteries were established. The **Brownsville** National Cemetery was located within the confines of Fort Brown, TX. In 1909, the Army post was abandoned. The Army contracted with a private firm to have the remains that were buried in the Brownsville National Cemetery transferred to the **Alexandria** National Cemetery in Pineville, LA. In 1868, national cemeteries were established at **Barrancas**, FL; **Fort Gibson**, OK; and **Little Rock**, AR, as well as at **Chalmette**, LA. Chalmette is operated and maintained by the Department of the Interior. By 1870, the number of national cemeteries reached 73.

Remembering our Veterans

May 1938: "Flags will be placed on the graves of 652 departed war veterans in 56 cemeteries in Clark County on Memorial Day, May 30. There are a number of other Civil War veterans buried in unmarked graves, whose identities have not been established. Of the deceased veterans, five served in the War of 1812, two in the Mexican War, 473 in the Civil War, one in Indian Wars, 32 in the Spanish-American War and 136 in World War I. A number of men served in two wars. Buried in Clark County are veterans of every war the United States has ever been engaged in except the Revolutionary War..." *Clark County Press, Neillsville, WI, May 1938*

Area Cemeteries of Greenwood, Wisconsin

Beaver Township

Greenwood City

Forest Hill. Braun Settlement

Weston West

Chapel Hill
(Formerly Weston East)

Warner UCC East

Warner UCC West

114

GREENWOOD, WI CITY CEMETERY CIVIL WAR BURIALS

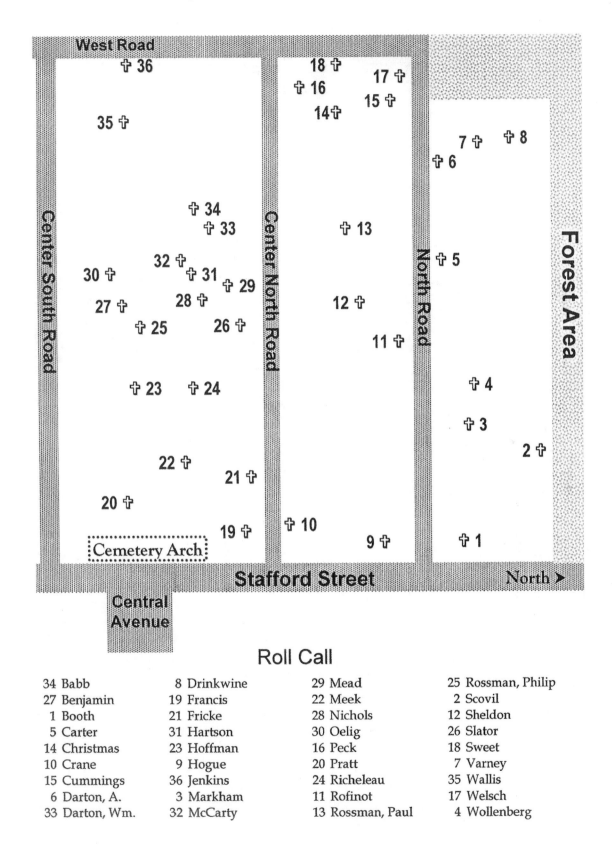

Roll Call

34 Babb	8 Drinkwine	29 Mead	25 Rossman, Philip
27 Benjamin	19 Francis	22 Meek	2 Scovil
1 Booth	21 Fricke	28 Nichols	12 Sheldon
5 Carter	31 Hartson	30 Oelig	26 Slator
14 Christmas	23 Hoffman	16 Peck	18 Sweet
10 Crane	9 Hogue	20 Pratt	7 Varney
15 Cummings	36 Jenkins	24 Richeleau	35 Wallis
6 Darton, A.	3 Markham	11 Rofinot	17 Welsch
33 Darton, Wm.	32 McCarty	13 Rossman, Paul	4 Wollenberg

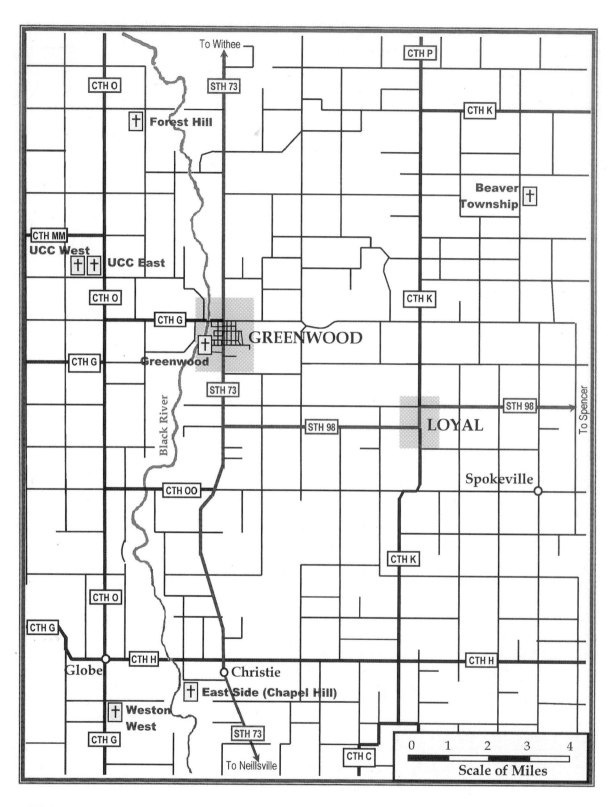

This symbol denotes the 7 cemetery locations associated with the Civil War Veteran burials in this book for Beaver, Eaton, Warner and Weston Townships,

Honoring our Civil War Veterans

Curtis Markham Marker Dedication, 17 Jun 2006, Greenwood, WI City Cemetery

Left: Co. B, 2nd WI Civil War "Re-enactors." Bugler John Dudkiewicz plays "Lights Out," the final call of the night for the Infantry and "Taps," the last call of the night for the Cavalry.
Right: Greenwood American Legion Color Guard at their stone dedication for Civil War Veteran, Curtis Markham.

A Special "Thank You" to the Greenwood American Legion for their dedication to placing cemetery markers for the Veterans of the Civil War who are buried in Greenwood, WI.

July 4, 2006, Thorp, WI City Cemetery

Over 20 new Civil War markers were dedicated by the Thorp American Legion and the Clark Co., WI History Buffs. Re-Enactors Fired the Cannon which actually shook the ground all 3 times it was shot. The Main address was given by American Legion State Vice Commander, Don Schindler, who told the mythical story of "Taps".

Greenwood, WI Volunteers

(Left Photo) In the early spring, Burton Jolivette, Commander of the American Legion, received a $500 check from the Chamber of Commerce to help defray the cost of the new Civil War Grave markers.
L-R: Burton Jolivette, Vicki Sterland, Treasurer, Pat Lindner President of the Greenwood Chamber of Commerce and Dick Adler, Finance Officer for the Greenwood American Legion.

(Right Photo) Members of the Greenwood American Legion cleaned all of the existing markers in preparation for the August 8, 2009 Dedication Program.
L-R: Dick Adler, Lloyd Horn and Al Schneider

History of Taps
"Taps" – Twenty-four Notes on a Bugle

Of all the military bugle calls, none is so easily recognized or renders deeper emotion than Taps. Up to the Civil War, the traditional call at day's end was a tune, borrowed from the French called Lights Out. It was mid-summer and the Union and Confederate armies had been fighting for seven long days. Brigadier General Daniel Adams Butterfield was serving as commander of a brigade of the Fifth Corps of the Army of the Potomac. The fighting had been brutal and the troops on each side had suffered considerable loss. At that time, the only efficient way for leaders to communicate with their troops was with the use of bugle calls designated for specific purposes. There were calls for charge, retreat, lights out, and other orders.

In July of 1862, in the aftermath of the bloody Seven Days battles at Harrison's Landing in Virginia, hard on the loss of 600 men and wounded himself, Brigadier General Daniel Adams Butterfield called the brigade bugler to his tent. He thought "Lights Out" was too formal and he wished to honor his men. Oliver Wilcox Norton, the bugler, tells the story, *"...showing me some notes on a staff written in pencil on the back of an envelope, (he) asked me to sound them on my bugle. I did this several times, playing the music as written. He changed it somewhat, lengthening some notes and shortening others, but retaining the melody as he first gave it to me. After getting it to his satisfaction, he directed me to sound that call for Taps thereafter in place of the regulation call. The music was beautiful on that still summer night and was heard far beyond the limits of our Brigade. The next day I was visited by several buglers from neighboring Brigades, asking for copies of the music which I gladly furnished. The call was gradually taken up through the Army of the Potomac."*

The bugle call was initially intended to signal the setting of the sun, but the tradition of playing "Taps" at military funerals began very shortly after its composition. Captain John C. Tidball, of the Union Army, was charged with supervising the burial of his cannoneer killed in action during the Peninsular Campaign at Harrison's Landing. At that time, the custom was to fire three rifle shots over the grave at the close of the funeral service. But Tidball's troops were concealed in the woods in an advanced position. He feared that the firing of three volleys so near enemy forces, might renew fighting and so decided to substitute the sounding of "Taps" as a tribute to the fallen comrade.

The more emotive and powerful Taps was soon adopted throughout the military. Taps was officially recognized by the U.S. Army in 1874. It became standard at military funeral ceremonies in 1891. There is something singularly beautiful and appropriate in the music of this wonderful call. Its strains are melancholy, yet full of rest and peace. Its echoes linger in the heart long after its tones have ceased to vibrate in the air.

Taps is played nightly at 10 PM (2200 hrs) in military installations at non-deployed locations to indicate that it is "lights out." When Taps is played at a funeral, it is customary to salute if in uniform, or to place the right hand over the heart if out of uniform.

TAPS

The original version was purely instrumental; the following is one of the later sets of lyrics written for the musical score.

Day is done, gone the sun
From the lake, from the hill,
From the sky
All is well, safely rest, God is nigh

Go to sleep, peaceful sleep,
May the soldier or sailor God keep.
On the land or the deep,
Safe in sleep.

Thanks and praise for our days
'neath the sky.
As we go, this we know.
God is nigh

Silver Taps Students who die while currently enrolled at Texas A&M are honored at Silver Taps. The song is played three times: once to the north, once to the south, and once to the west. It is never played to the east, "because the sun will never rise on that student again".

Echo Taps is a tradition at American military schools, and is played at 2300 (11:00) when a member or former member of a school's Corps of Cadets is killed in action. The bugler on the south end plays the first 3 notes of Silver Taps and the bugler on the north end echoes; the bugler on the south end plays the next 3 notes and is echoed for the rest of the song.

Grand Review, Washington, D.C., 23-24 May 1865
Union Victory Celebration